# THE
# MESSIAH
## AND THE END OF THIS
# WORLD

## BEN AMMI

Published by
Communicators Press
P.O. Box 26063, Washington, D.C. 20001
(202) 726-8618
FAX (202) 291-9149

**ISBN** 0-9620463-3-7

Library of Congress Catalog Card Number
91-076545

The scriptural references used in this book are taken
from the New Scofield Reference Bible

# Table Of Contents

# FOREWORD

There have been numerous doomsday, "end-of-the-world" clair-voyants that have emerged on the scene in our generation, and probably in every generation since the time of Noah. Most of the foretellers of the forthcoming destruction of the earth haven't received (nor merited) any extraordinary attention. However, it's hard to deny the imminent threat to the world today after the vast arsenal of destruction that was displayed during the Gulf War. And even if that didn't get you to thinking about the "end", if you seriously consider the vast amount of social devastation and destruction that exists today - sexual perversion, AIDS, mounting divorce, crime, drugs, unwed motherhood, racism, sexism, and much, much more - then you have to believe that if Gor-bachev or Bush don't push "the button", God surely will. Therefore, if you are sober-minded in most things, Ben Ammi's book, The <u>Messiah and the End of the World</u>, should make you sit up and take notice of the world around you. Ben Ammi's prediction that the end of this world is imminent does not imply that the earth and all the creations will be totally annihilated. It's quite ludicrous to entertain the thought that the wicked could destroy all of creation, even though it appears as if they have the means to do so. Only the God that created the earth can destroy it.

> *"For thus saith the Lord that created the heavens; God himself that formed the earth and made it; he hath established it, he created it not in vain, he formed it to be inhabited; I am the Lord; and there is none else."*

**Isaiah 45:18**

This reference is explicitly concerning the end of an age - the world of the Euro-gentiles. In this book, Ben Ammi explains how the presence of the African Hebrews at Jerusalem signifies the end of the rule of the Euro-gentiles upon this planet. His version of the end of <u>this</u> world warrants special consideration for several reasons.

First, he is a former Black American, presently living in Jerusalem; that alone is a phenomenon. Secondly, if we take into account his actual

ii

experience for the last twenty-three years, his credibility to predict the end of this world would be further substantiated. In 1967, he led more than 300 Americans into the interior jungle of Liberia, where they remained for nearly three years. Afterwards, he guided a little better than a third of that number on to the Holy Land - Israel - to establish the prophetic Kingdom of God, an event that was prophesied in Daniel 2:44. His credibility as a predictor is enhanced by virtue of the fact that the platform of his prediction is Jerusalem, the Spiritual Center of the world, the home of the prophets.

And finally, just as Yeshua (Jesus) was looked upon as an outcast, rebel and reject by the established religious and political order of his day, likewise Ben Ammi (being a member of the rejected "negro" race) is similarly despised by this world's rulers.

> *"Who hath believed our report? And to whom is the arm of the Lord revealed?*
>
> *For he shall grow up before him as a tender plant, and as a root out of dry ground: he hath no form nor comeliness; and when we shall see him, there is no beauty that we should desire him.*
>
> *He is despised and rejected of men; a man of sorrows, and acquainted with grief; and we hid as it were our faces from him; he was despised, and we esteemed him not."*

**Isaiah 53:1-3**

The writings that you are about to read are extraordinarily different from the norm. In this work, Ben Ammi illuminates the revelations of the prophets, and with ease unravels their profound writings. The prophets - the men of God who moved by faith to inscribe the indelible words of the Holy One of Israel - were obviously aware that they would not see the end of this wicked world in the flesh but their unyielding allegiance to God inspired them on.

Ben Ammi resurrects the spirits of these awesome men of God and causes them to live again in our midst. His scholarly understanding of the Holy tongue (Hebrew) strengthens his ability to explain and clarify more profoundly the words, idioms and parables of these ancient Hebrew scribes whose writings have often been distorted by the trans-

iii

lators (who compiled what is known today as the King James Version of the Bible) and misinterpreted by the layman. Every passage by Ben Ammi is explicit, giving greater clarity, distinction and strength to the Holy writings. He explains in simplicity the plan and purpose of the God of Creation and all that relates to Him, as if he has a direct line to His Holy abode.

He masterfully elucidates the Word of God and instructs how it is to be used as the ultimate weapon against the evil one - satan. He delineates the Truth and the lie and explains their effect upon us in our everyday lives and activities. He spares nothing or no one that is guilty of transgression of God's will. He expounds upon the indiscriminate nature of the Truth and reveals how it frees those imprisoned; it is revealed unto all that seek it and is known to those that find it.

Contrary to a lie, which is deceptive, misleading and seductive, Truth shines as a star - unadulterated and undefiled - as an invincible warrior ready to free all those that are bound. As Ben Ammi's words unfold, you be the judge of whether they are the Truth, because the Truth invigorates, stimulates and resurrects the soul. All that seek Truth will hear it and will adhere to nothing else. Yeshua (Jesus) said, "My sheep shall hear my voice and a stranger they shall not follow." The Master Teacher only meant that Truth is universal and impossible to be misinterpreted.

Ben Ammi brings God down from the sky (the abstract) where the theological teachings of Europe have transplanted Him. In doing so, he causes us to see evermore clearly the "path" that leads to God and the proper way to develop a harmonious relationship with Him. He gives us the keys which will ultimately influence the realization of the absolute life, the life which only a minute few of the world's inhabitants, past and present, have ever experienced. They are the keys to the world to come...with the end of this world.

**Prince Gavriel HaGadol**
**April 1991**

iv

# A Note To Our Readers

You will frequently encounter the use of the term "Euro-gentile" throughout this work. It is a term coined by the African Hebrew Israelites in keeping with our having seized the "Power to Define," a concept which was discussed in detail in the book, <u>God The Black Man And Truth</u>."

The suffix "gentile" simply denotes a people or nation that is without the knowledge of the True and Living God of Creation. When using the term "Euro-gentile," (often interchangeably with "Euro-American"), we are in fact referring to the entire European family of nations; i.e., Europe, the United States of America, Canada, South Africa, New Zealand, Australia, etc.

Its usage also reflects the pervasive and powerful social, economic, cultural and political influence these nations have wielded on this planet. As such, though these "Euro-gentile" nations are obviously and unquestionably responsible for having brought all of humanity and creation to the brink of destruction as a result of their continuously evil activities and deeds, no racist or otherwise negative connotations are inferred by the phrase.

You will also notice the capitalization of the word "black," when referring to race, as opposed to merely color. We are well aware that this usage may not conform to generally-accepted norms of the English language.

While the use of "Black" may thus be deemed inaccurate, it must be recognized that many "Blacks" or "Africans" have not yet arrived to the point of tracing and identifying their particular nation of origin, or nationality. It is an obvious fact that our skins are black and that "Black Americans" hail collectively from the continent of Africa.

Again, many other words and terms may be capitalized; e.g., "Truth," "Divine," "Love," or "Power to Define." When they appear in such formal usage, it denotes their application as a principle "building block" or concept in the New World Order.

# Introduction

Throughout the pages of this work with the help and guidance of the Most High, I will clarify some crucial concepts that are very significant in our quest for God. I only ask that you read truly seeking to understand without preconceived ideas. Then, in your final analysis, be fair with yourself for the sake of yourself.

The decisions that confront our generations are in most cases not easy ones, but they are the decisions that will determine if the coming generations will even have a place on this planet earth. How long do we have? In 1990 major networks and magazines declared that the earth has become an endangered species. If an enemy of the planet was testing public reaction, he was certainly encouraged by the reticence of the public's response. Such a response could only hasten the movement of the ominous clouds of destruction.

You must be made consciously aware that the greatest period of change the world has experienced since the fall of Adam is on the horizon. This transition will not involve science and technology in major roles. They will be relegated to the status of guilty bystanders. This transition will be spiritual - an obvious, evident confrontation between God and satan, or the rise of right and the fall of wrong. In addition to that, Africa and African Americans will be the central figures during this season of world purification. The Euro-gentile world today is a paradox: prosperity and abundance surrounded by turmoil and confusion - good and evil. Such a world is ripe for a comforting delusion about the future and the primary reason that the age of transition will catch the great majority of the earth's inhabitants by surprise. I have continuously warned the apathetic human family of the imminent dangers of their hypnotic pursuit of materialism. Take heed, for when the final phase begins, it will be virtually too late to escape, for the end will come upon you as a snare. My exegesis on the end of this world is to awaken you from your comatose relationship with evil. It is time to move. You cannot afford to take a "wait-and-see" attitude when so much, as a matter of fact - everything - is at stake. Daniel the Prophet warns: "The multitudes of them that sleep in the dust of the earth shall awake, some to everlasting life, and some to shame and everlasting contempt." The choice is up to you. You should be making a sincere effort to erect God's protective shield around yourself, your household and all who will give ear to the spirit of Godly reasoning.

My dissertation on the end of this world does not begin with atomic weapons and chemical warheads. When those weapons are used at the end of the age, it will be <u>after</u> the end of this, the Euro-American, Euro-gentile world. Many writers have connected the use of such weapons to the end of life on the planet earth. My emphasis is on the end that will come as a thief in the night; the one that you won't hear them explaining...the end that will trap the inhabitants in the house that is engulfed in the fiery flames of God's judgment.

Reflect upon the season when Noah preached an imminent end of the era and world in which he lived. He saw a social condition in existence or approaching that was to be equated as an end in itself. When Yeshua (Jesus) said the end of this present world was to be as in the days of Noah, he was basing his statement as equated by the state of the people's relationship with God, environment (nature), social corruption and evil imagination which would ultimately equal the end. This is the primary reason that you are warned to watch, listen, and study the words of the inspired prophets of God. Remember the thief in the night is most effective when you're not watching, listening or protected by God. The chemistry or mixture of elements that caused the end of Noah's world was not the rain that brought about the flood. To say that the rain destroyed the ancient world is a euphemism. The rain was merely washing it all away; it did not in itself cause the end of the world. The rain came after the end of the world. I then see the equation which equals the end of this world swiftly approaching.

Thus inspired by a merciful God, I am calling your attention to the season at hand. The words I've scribed are Truth. Be not angry with me, because I've spoken the Truth unto you, for without Truth, you have no chance to change and live.

This world is being destroyed by greed-motivated Euro-gentile science, technology and evil inventions. There has been an accelerated global rift in the last twenty-five years: the separation of sanity (the

# Introduction

slower, under-developed world) from insanity (the fast, developed world) because of race and an illusion of superiority. A "world" has completely detached itself from nine-tenths of the earth's people. Yet its image is tempting and deceptive, casting a dark shadow over all nations, leading them away from humanity at a break-neck speed. Thinking they have become wise, they are entering a vacuum, trapped in space. They are so far out in front until they're becoming extinct. God has worked a magnificent miracle by virtually disconnecting this world from the human family. Whereas the slow world isn't really slow; it is in the process of becoming a new world by necessity. It is the end of this fast world that is in sight.

It appears as if the future is passing the third world or poorer regions by. But the truth is that their future depends upon them letting the fast world pass by. The warnings are to prevent the slow nations from coupling with the world that is ending. To remain aloof from them is the blessing, not the curse. The fast world is trapped; they can't turn back to the slow world, and to continue on their present path will be their destruction. The new world will represent a return to sanity, for the fast world has gone mad. The new world will be required to revolutionize their concept of progress and development, re-emphasizing the eternal need for God, people and the creation, not science, technology and inventions.

I also touch upon the great deception that has been wrought through a very innocuous-appearing educational process. I always stress that education in Euro-gentile institutions is relevant to the intent. Remember that this hell on earth was fashioned by and governed by educated men. The major problems facing the human family today were caused by the educated, not the uneducated, causing us to acknowledge that while education lies at the heart of society, it must be right education.

What has gone wrong when man is inert on the vital issues concerning his future existence? All of man's troubles can be traced back to his beginning; they are spiritual in nature. That implies a problem between two directions: one right, and the other wrong. On this sordid path they are fed an unholy diet of materialism. The materialistic diet never satiates the appetite; it merely creates greater lust (greed). These inanimate objects cause man to always be discontent, and soon he is possessed with greed, the end result of trying to solve a spiritual problem through materialistic attainments.

*"He that loveth silver shall not be satisfied with silver, nor he that loveth abundance, with increase; this is also vanity."*

**Ecclesiastes 5:10**

No man can serve two masters; neither can a spiritual problem be solved by inanimate materialism, and no materialistic greed can be satiated spiritually. The solution: the Living God has to come alive in you and Truth has to become your friend. In your fallen state you regressed into a degenerate image actively carrying out the will of satan. Humanity has to now submit and be fashioned again in the image and likeness of God.

The Hebraic concept of image and likeness conveys representation/ representative and similitude. Through the spirit of God, man was to be the representative and similitude of God on earth. The hour is late, judgment day or the Day of the Lord has come. The decision is rectification or extinction.

In Chapter I, I attempt to remove the contemporary Euro-centric Jesus and focus the mind again on the African Hebrew Messiah of 2000 years ago, showing the difference between Michelangelo's Jesus and the Biblical Yeshua. Many Black Biblical scholars are aware of the great Biblical deception that has been wrought by European-Euro-American scholars influenced by racist overtones. Nevertheless, they still fear to clearly identify the major characters being used by God as being of the Black race. They very meticulously identify the minor players, but the ingrained inferiority complex causes them to leave the major roles for Europeans. Where that is not the case, then they leave room for sufficient speculation from which the same conclusions are inevitable.

Needless to say, this book is not targeting Biblical history as its primary subject. Howbeit, those capable and qualified historians that continue to shirk their responsibilities to the human family must be taken to task. I need not be a historian to know that the Bible from Genesis to Malachi is a recorded history of Africa and Africans, Black men and women in

# Introduction

transition after their fall from God's graces. Linguistically, I've substituted the correct "Yeshua", the name of the carpenter from Nazareth, son of Joseph and Mary. Initially, you may find it somewhat awkward to adjust to, but if you overcome the initial sensitivity and fear, you will find that new horizons of strength and understanding will be your reward.

The Bible, as an indispensable tool of liberation, has to be reassessed in the light of ancient truth instead of contemporary deception. There will be no world of tomorrow without a truthful, reassessment of our world of yesterday. As we return to Biblical truth and away from contemporary religion, we will discover that neither Yeshua nor the Apostles had any preconceived notion of establishing a new dogma or religion, but to fulfill the true mission of an old one.

I have included some photo-replicas of famous paintings for your perusal. I ask that you study the character and motif. In so doing, you will discover that there isn't even the slightest aura of Holiness, only Euro-gentile artistic fantasy. Upon close examination you will find vulgarity and the archetype of Euro-American, Euro-gentile distorted Biblical idealism.

The other chapters paint a picture of a Judgment Day that has already begun and is approaching the apocalyptical climax.

I have placed the African American on center stage in the process of redemption in which, much to his surprise, he will be playing the major role. This world is destined to be destroyed by fire. I was taught this since my early childhood, but I was not taught that God is a consuming fire. Subsequently, I was not aware of the role of the Truth and the Word of God in this intensive heated struggle.

*"For the Lord thy God is a consuming fire, even a jealous God."*

**Deuteronomy 4:24**

God has promised that some would be purified by the fire, while others will be consumed. Finally, when the fiery bombs fall, Judgment Day will have passed and the earth's purification will have begun. All of those holding fast to a lie at that time will be trapped in everlasting torment caused by the effect of awesome evil weapons.

I beseech you to hear this doctrine of the Kingdom, for only these words can form your shield of protection from the unprecedented physical plagues that are to come upon this evil generation.

# About The Author

*Ben Ammi (which means "Son of My People" in Hebrew) was born October 12, 1939, to Levi and Rena Carter, in an old, dilapidated neighborhood on the near southwest side of Chicago, Illinois. I first met Ben in the fall of 1948, when his family moved into my neighborhood on Chicago's near northwest side, several blocks from Lake Michigan. From that day on, our lives have been intertwined, as we never lived far apart. We grew together and shared our hopes and dreams for the future.*

*Much of our youth was spent a block or so from the old Cabrini (now the notorious Cabrini-Green) housing projects. An extraordinary person from his youth, Ben always had an intense and boundless love for his God, people, and the Creation. In the forty-two years that I have known him, I've yet to see him in any violent, physical confrontation (which was a phenomenon in our neighborhood), even though he was a state-wide wrestling champion. His strength was and is his unique insight and the precision of his tongue. He has an exceptional ability to discern and articulate. In this he has no equal -- and I'm not being partial. It seems as though there has always been some "unseen force" watching over him.*

*Ben attended Washburn Trade School, later transferring to Marshall High where he dropped out during his third year. He joined the U.S. Army, serving on a nearby missile base. Still, he managed to complete his high school education during his military term. Shortly thereafter, he married and found employment at Howard Foundry, where he became an excellent metallurgist.*

*It was during this period that Ben met his first mentor of Hebrew history, the elder Eliyahoo Buie, who taught him in-depth concerning our African Hebrew heritage. Elder Buie confirmed many things passed on to Ben verbally by his parents and relatives, inspiring his avid search into the Holy Scriptures for the hidden truths concerning the agonizing captivity of the African in America.*

*Perplexed by the overt racial injustice of American society, and the "privileged position" of Europeans in America, he questioned whether in fact God was somehow partial to them. Looking upon the despair of his people, he reasoned: "If 'thy will be done' indeed means the inevitable manifestation of God's will -- then the horrible predicament of the Black man in America must be the Will of God."*

*Intense meditation, study and research soon convinced him that the problems of African Americans were self-inflicted -- the result of their willful disobedience and not God's ultimate will. He then set out to strengthen his personal relationship with the God of Israel, seeking to invoke His presence in the struggle for true freedom on behalf of Black people in America, and all men in general.*

*A co-founder of the Abeta Hebrew Cultural Center on Chicago's south side, he became one of the center's chief teachers, spokesmen, and organizers. Here he had the vision that an exodus of the Black man from the United States was inevitable, and indeed necessary, if true freedom was ever to be attained.*

*In 1967, at the zenith of the Black revol. in America, approximately 350 men, women and children left the confines of the United States enroute to Israel, via Liberia, West Africa. After a successful sojourn of two-and-one-half years in the interior of Liberia, where a myriad of negative and unbecoming traits were purged, the remnant of these pioneers moved on to Israel in 1969. Since that time, Ben Ammi and his followers have struggled to establish the long-waited Kingdom of God -- on earth!*

*Ben Ammi has boldly taken on the prophetic mandate to lead all men -- in word and deed -- back unto God. His burning pursuit of Divine Intellect and Wisdom has qualified him to be the master teacher and profound (yet simple) philosopher that he is. Multi-lingual, he communicates the Plan of God to others clearly and effectively with the understanding of the original Hebrew thought. As spiritual leader and Father of the African Hebrew Israelites, Ben Ammi has become the first to successfully bring about the repatriation of African Americans. He is beloved by his people, admired by his acquaintances and respected by his foes. His selfless regard for the well-being of others makes him a natural leader. Ben Ammi exudes supreme confidence and composure, seemingly unshaken by opposition and the many obstacles encountered along the way. His record demands the serious attention of all.*

*All praises to the Most High God of Israel!*

*Prince Gavriel HaGadol*

*"And the great dragon was cast out, that old serpent, called the devil, and satan, which deceiveth the whole world:"*

**Revelations 12:9**

# DECEIVE

*To cause to accept as true or valid what is false and invalid; to lead astray; to mislead*

*painting by Michelangelo*

XV

*painting by Hunnaeus*

xvi

*painting entitled "Crucifixion" by Titian*

*painting by Michelangelo*

xviii

*painting entitled "The Comforting" by Hoffman*

The Euro-gentile gave you the idea of an inferiority complex in your early childhood, even before you could read. Children receive their first worldly images and impressions from pictures. Therefore, before you could read, you opened the Bible, and from the pictures you received your first impression of God and angels, and you have never forgotten what you saw. You saw pictures of a European Jesus on the cross, a European Jesus carrying the cross, and teaching the people on the Mount of Olives. You saw a picture of a European Mary, the mother of Jesus, and you saw pictures of angels in negligees with wings on their backs. You saw many other pictures of Europeans being cast in the surroundings of the Holy Land. As you grew up, you never realized that it was those childhood thoughts of Euro-gentiles as God that started you on the path of attempting to prove yourself worthy and acceptable to Europeans. He has portrayed himself as God having both your future and your destiny in his hands.

They kept the pictures (thoughts) before you all of your life, everywhere you went, in every store in every home, and on almost every wall of your church. Now you even feel offended when someone suggests that the pictures be taken down and destroyed. When someone mentions the racist connotation of these pictures to European Christians or others, the favorite answer is "God doesn't have any color." And, worse yet, he turns around and implies that the one who raises the question is a racist.

Why is it that the problem of race only enters the picture when we begin discussing positive Black images? How could it be that all of these artists have had such a vivid imagination of all those characters being European, but none of them have ever imagined that those African Hebrews in that African land (Israel) were Black?

**God the Black Man and Truth**

xx

# Introductory Study Material

The following scriptural references and etymological notes are to assist and enhance your understanding of the subject matter of the first chapter. In order to better understand "The Rise of the Messiah" chapter, it will be necessary to refer back to these notes as you read the Hebraic Messianic concepts. These words will provide you with immediate reference material, and greatly assist your honest search for a better, more lucid understanding of what you now believe in and hope for.

We must take into consideration that when the Holy One of Israel brought forth the Messianic vision, His adversary , satan, put forth the Messianic conspiracy. Now, at this very late hour, trying to make the way straight after generations of deception is more than a notion. The Messianic person was to be the light of salvation. The conspiracy put salvation far up in the sky -- made it an unknown quality in an unknown place. Now the messengers and message of God have to bring it back down to earth.

Salvation in the prophetic dissertation is conceptualized as: deliverance; victory over the forces that oppose God, His creation, and His image. But to simplify the above-mentioned and to land it right smack in your dining room parlor, salvation in its quintessence is centered around your health and welfare, which once again causes you to focus in on your entire way of life. God's message of deliverance never leaves you hanging in space. It keeps you concentrating on the day-to-day realities of your own works and activities, explaining how they will influence the ultimate victory.

The Messiah's message will in most cases be greatly influenced by the health and welfare of His/the people. After the effects of the conspiracy, a proclaimed Deliverer or Savior who expresses his concern over the dietary habits and the world view would appear too common, not sufficiently ostentatious and pompous. Using health, welfare and victory as the measuring rods to determine if the force of true salvation exists in the midst of those called African Americans, we find: health in a constant state of deterioration; welfare (what has a man gained if he profiteth the whole world and loseth/has lost his soul?) and victory over the forces of evil, a force that most African Americans don't even recognize as a tangible element. Why are they so far from salvation? Because they're waiting for the Savior conceptualized, defined and described by their captors, subconsciously rejecting all others.

**Note:** *Throughout the following scriptures, the author has interjected commentary or more detailed explanations to further clarify for the reader the true meaning. These portions will be capitalized and delineated by brackets.*

## *Sanctifying*     *Anointing*     *Consecrating*

*"And the Lord said unto Samuel, How long wilt thou mourn for Saul, seeing I have rejected him from reigning over Israel? Fill thine horn with oil, and go, I will send thee to Jesse the Bethlemite; for I have provided me a king among his sons.*

*And Samuel said, How can I go? If Saul hear it, he will kill me. And the Lord said, Take an heifer with thee, and say, I am come to sacrifice to the Lord.*

*And call Jesse to the sacrifice, and I will show thee what thou shalt do; and thou shalt anoint unto me him whom I name unto thee. And Samuel did that which the Lord spake, and came to Bethlehem. And the elders of the town trembled at his coming, and said, Comest thou peaceably?*

*And he said, Peaceably; I am come to sacrifice unto the Lord. Sanctify yourselves, and come with me to the sacrifice. And he sanctified Jesse and his sons, and called them to the sacrifice. And it came to pass, when they were come, that he looked on Eliab and said, Surely the Lord's anointed* [MAH-SHE-AHK IS WRITTEN IN HEBREW = MESSIAH (ENGLISH) OR CHRIST (OS) (GREEK). THUS A MORE ACCURATE UNDERSTANDING OF THIS PASSAGE WOULD BE "SURELY THE LORD'S MESSIAH OR CHRIST..."] *is before him.*

*But the Lord said unto Samuel, Look not on his countenance, or on the height of his stature, because I have refused him; for the*

2

*Lord seeth not as man seeth; for man looketh on the outward appearance, but the Lord looketh on the heart.*

*Then Jesse called Abinadab, and made him pass before Samuel. And he said, Neither hath the Lord chosen this one. Then Jesse made Shammah to pass by. And he said, Neither hath the Lord chosen this one.*

*Again, Jesse made seven of his sons to pass before Samuel. And Samuel said unto Jesse, the Lord hath not chosen these. And Samuel said unto Jesse, Are here all thy children? And he said, there remaineth yet the youngest, and, behold, he keepeth the sheep. And Samuel said unto Jesse, Send and fetch him; for we will not sit down til he come hither.*

*And he sent, and brought him in. Now he was ruddy, and withal of a beautiful countenance, and goodly to look to. And the Lord said, Arise,* <u>anoint</u> *him;* [MAKE HIM A MESSIANIC PER-SONAGE.] *for this is he.*

*Then Samuel took the horn of oil, and* <u>anointed</u> *him in the midst of his brethren: and* <u>the Spirit of the Lord</u> *came upon David from that day forward."* [CONSIDER HERE THE WORDS OF ISAIAH THE PROPHET: "THE SPIRIT OF THE LORD GOD IS UPON ME: BECAUSE THE LORD HATH ANOINTED ME TO PREACH GOOD TIDINGS UNTO THE MEEK;"...]

**I Samuel 16:1-13**

*"*<u>The Spirit of the Lord</u> *God is upon me; because the Lord hath* <u>anointed</u> *me to preach good tidings unto the meek; he hath sent me to bind up the broken-hearted, to proclaim liberty to the captives, and the opening of the prison to them that are bound;* [THIS IS THE CONDENSED VERSION OF THE MES-SIANIC MISSION AS GIVEN TO THE INDIVIDUAL(S) AND PASSED ON TO THOSE WHO WOULD BECOME THE MESSIANIC PEOPLE.]

*To proclaim the acceptable year of the Lord, and the day of vengeance of our God; to comfort all that mourn."*

**Isaiah 61:1-2**

# Anointed (<u>Messianic</u>) Personages And Their Dejection

**NOTE:** *In each instance the underlined is written Mah-she-ahk in Hebrew = Messiah (English), Christos (Greek).*

*And David said to Abishai, Destroy him not; for who can stretch forth his hand against the Lord's anointed, and be guiltless?"*

*The Lord forbid that I should stretch forth mine hand against the <u>Lord's anointed</u>: but, I pray thee, take thou now the spear that is at his bolster, and the cruse of water, and let us go."*

*"This thing is not good that thou hast done. As the Lord liveth, ye are worthy to die, because ye have not kept your master, the <u>Lord's anointed</u>. And now see where the king's spear is, and cruse of water that was at his bolster."*

*"The Lord render to every man his righteousness and his faithfulness: for the Lord delivered thee into my hand to day, but I would not stretch forth mine hand against the <u>Lord's anointed</u>."*

**I Samuel 26: 9, 11, 16, 23**

*"Now these be the last words of David. David, the son of Jesse said, and the man who was raised up on high, <u>the anointed of the God of Jacob</u>, and the sweet psalmist of Israel, said,"...*

**II Samuel 23:1**

*"And thine house and thy kingdom shall be established for ever before thee: thy throne shall be established for ever."*

**II Samuel 7:16**

4

# The Messiah and the End of this World

*"Who hath believed our report? And to whom is the arm of the Lord revealed?*

*For he shall grow up before him as a tender plant, and as a root out of a dry ground: he hath no form nor comeliness; and when we shall see him, there is no beauty that we should desire him.*

*He is despised and rejected of men; a man of sorrows; and acquainted with grief: and we hid as it were our faces from him; he was despised, and we esteemed him not.*

*Surely he hath borne out griefs, and carried our sorrows: yet we did esteem him stricken, smitten of God, and afflicted.*

*But he was wounded for our transgressions, he was bruised for our iniquities: the chastisement of our peace was upon him; and with his stripes we are healed.*

*All we like sheep have gone astray; we have turned every one to his own way; and the Lord hath laid on him the iniquity of us all. He was oppressed, and he was afflicted, yet he opened not his mouth: he is brought as a lamb to the slaughter, and as a sheep before her shearers is dumb, so he openeth not his mouth.*

*He was taken from prison and from judgment: and who shall declare his generation? For he was cut off out of the land of the living: for the transgression of my people he was stricken.*

*And he made his grave with the wicked, and with the rich in his death; because he had done no violence, neither was any deceit in his mouth.*

*Yet it pleased the Lord to bruise him; he hath put him to grief; when thou shalt make his soul an offering for sin, he shall see his seed, he shall prolong his days and the pleasure of the Lord shall prosper in his hand."*

**Isaiah 53:1-10**

*"The Lord called thy name, A green olive tree, fair, and of goodly fruit; with the noise of a great tumult he hath kindled fire upon it, and the branches of it are broken.*

*For the Lord of hosts, that planted thee, hath pronounced evil against thee, for the evil of the house of Israel and of the house of Judah, which they have done against themselves to provoke me to anger in offering incense unto Baal.*

*And the Lord hath given me knowledge of it, and I know it; then thou showedst me their doings.*

*But I was like a lamb or an ox that is brought to the slaughter; and I knew not that they devised devices against me, saying, Let us destroy the tree with the fruit thereof, and let us cut him off from the land of the living, that his name may be no more remembered."*

**Jeremiah 11:16-19**

In reviewing the above scriptures, please note the similarity of Jeremiah's anguish and Isaiah's general Messianic sorrows. This helps to substantiate that the scriptural references to the calling and suffering of the Messianic individual are not a description of one historical figure. They are elucidating and giving us a better understanding of the one spirit of a/the chosen anointed messenger(s) that was/were consecrated for a special mission and service unto God throughout the generations. This means that it is a reflection of the lives of an entire lineage of individuals whose calling and experiences were/will be similar. They were/could be applied to the Messiah in whatever generation he appeared. To reinforce this concept, one would need only to read the many Psalms wherein David pours out his soul before the throne of God because of the continuous trials and tribulation he experienced as a Messianic king over Israel.

## *Anointed*      Messianic Nation      *Consecrated*

*"Which covenant he made* with Abraham, *and his oath* unto Isaac;

*And confirmed the same* unto Jacob *for a law,* and to Israel *for an everlasting covenant:*

6

*Saying, Unto thee will I give the land of Canaan, the lot of your inheritance:*

*When they were but a few men in number; yea, very few, and strangers in it.*

*When they went from one nation to another, from one kingdom to another people;*

*He suffered no man do them wrong: yea, he reproved kings for their sakes;*

*Saying, Touch not mine anointed,* [HERE WE NOTE THAT IN HEBREW THE WORD MAH-SHE-AHK IS PLURAL-IZED: ME-SHE-KHY = MY MESSIAHS (ENGLISH), MY CHRISTS (GREEK). THIS IS A CASE OF BLATANT BEGUILEMENT BY USING THE INCORRECT ANOINTED WHICH COULD REFER TO AN IN-DIVIDUAL IN LIEU OF A NATION OF PEOPLE] *and do my prophets no harm."*

**Psalms 105:9-15**

*"And their seed shall be known among the Gentiles, and their offspring among the people: all that see them shall acknowledge them, that they are the seed which the Lord hath blessed."*

**Isaiah 61:9**

*"And in the days of these kings shall the God of heaven set up a kingdom, which shall never be destroyed: and the kingdom shall not be left to other people, but it shall break in pieces and consume all these kingdoms, and it shall stand for ever."*

**Daniel 2:44**

*"Thou sawest till that a stone was cut out without hands, which smote the image upon his feet that were of iron and clay, and broke them to pieces.*

*Then was the iron, the clay, the brass, the silver, and the gold, broken to pieces together, and became like the chaff of the summer*

7

*threshing floors; and the wind carried them away, that no place was found for them; and the stone that smote the image became a great mountain, and filled the whole earth."*

**Daniel 2:34-35**

*"These great beasts, which are four, are four kings, which shall arise out of the earth.*

*But the saints of the Most High shall take the kingdom and possess the kingdom for ever, even for ever and ever."*

*"I beheld, and the same horn made war with the saints, and prevailed against them;*

*Until the Ancient of days came, and judgment was given to the saints of the Most High, and the time came that the saints possessed the kingdom."*

*"And he shall speak great words against the Most High, and shall wear out the saints of the Most High, and think to change times and laws; and they shall be given into his hand until a time and times and the dividing of time.*

*But the judgment shall sit, and they shall take away his dominion, to consume and to destroy it unto the end.*

*And the kingdom and dominion, and the greatness of the kingdom under the whole heaven, shall be given to the people of the saints of the Most High, whose kingdom is an everlasting kingdom, and all dominions shall serve and obey him."*

**Daniel 7:17-18, 21-22, 25-27**

## *Anointed* <u>Messianic Individual And Nation</u>
### *Consecrated*

*"Listen, O isles, unto me; and hearken, ye people, from far; The Lord hath called me from the womb; from the bowels of my mother hath he made mention of my name.*

8

## The Messiah and the End of this World

*And he hath made my mouth like a sharp sword; in the shadow of his hand hath he hid me, and made me a polished shaft; in his quiver hath he hid me;*

*And said unto me, Thou art my servant, O Israel, in whom I will be glorified.*

*Then I said, I have labored in vain, I have spent my strength for nought, and in vain: yet surely my judgment is with the Lord, and my work with my God.*

*And now saith the Lord that formed me from the womb to be his servant, to bring Jacob again to him, Though Israel be not gathered, yet shall I be glorious in the eyes of the Lord, and my God shall be my strength.*

*And he said, It is a light thing that thou shouldest be my servant to raise up the tribes of Jacob, and to restore the preserved of Israel: I will also give thee for a light to the nations that thou mayest be my salvation unto the end of the earth."*

**Isaiah 49:1-6**

The following verses will also be of great assistance to you in furthering your understanding of Biblical similitudes. The authencity of the Messianic individual is affirmed and can only be confirmed through the Messianic Nation. He is an integral part of that nation from which he sprang forth. Take special note that the entire Nation of Israel is the Son of God. Therefore, in understanding this fact, we thus can remove any doubt as to whether a Son of God existed. This synergism strengthens the credibility of the individual and the Nation while neutralizing all destructive criticism and doubt.

Also, in the following scriptures we find a priestly similitude, wherein the entire Israelite Nation is cast into the role of priests. The anointed Messiah becomes a spiritual king/priest upon inheriting the throne of David. He is a priest born out of his relationship with the whole, therefore alleviating any controversy surrounding his being referred to as a king priest after the order of Melchizedek.

9

*When Israel was a child, then I loved him, and called my son out of Egypt."*

**Hosea 11:1**

*"And thou shalt say unto Pharoah, Thus saith the Lord, Israel is my son, even my firstborn.*

*And I say unto thee, Let my son go, that he may serve me; and if thou refuse to let him go, behold, I will slay thy son, even thy firstborn."*

**Exodus 4:22-23**

*"Now therefore, if ye will obey my voice indeed, and keep my covenant, then ye shall be a peculiar treasure unto me above all people; for all the earth is mine;*

*And ye shall be unto me a kingdom of priests, and an holy nation. These are the words which thou shalt speak unto the children of Israel."*

**Exodus 19:5-6**

*"But ye shall be named the Priests of the Lord; men shall call you the Ministers of our God; ye shall eat the riches of the Gentiles and in their glory shall ye boast yourselves."*

**Isaiah 61:6**

"Thus we see how the God of Creation, during His establishment of Divine Universal Order, brings forth man into a unique and specifically defined relationship to the world - and to the Godhead. Upon further examination, the aforementioned yields much understanding of the true intent of God concerning the true role of man. First, observe that the Creator did not deign to fashion man until the "sixth" day of the Divine creative cycle. Thus, man is not the primary creation. One might easily ask, "..why, if man was to ultimately be God's highest creation, was he not made first...?"

The answer, through discernment of the scripture itself, becomes obvious. The Creator brings forth a world of substance from His unlimited, Universal Consciousness and man, to whom "dominion" over this realm of substance is given, must necessarily be fashioned of this substance. For the Godhead, being pure Consciousness, imposed "image" and "likeness" upon a formless void, then, proceeding in an orderly fashion, orchestrated these forms into an ultimate expression, man. So that ones see in clear simplicity that the "dominion" given man is based upon his relationship to the substance, the physical world of which he is a part. By way of example, we recognize the shepard as such primarily by his relationship to his flock; we recognize the king as such by his relationship to his kingdom."

**God the Black Man and Truth**

This study chart is also to bring to your attention the portion of the Messianic conspiracy that pertains to names. We are focusing in on three languages: Hebrew, Greek and English, as they have played the dominant roles in Biblical translations. Approximately two thousand years ago, the Holy One of Israel ordained a messenger in the midst of His people, the Children of Israel. His name at birth was Yeshua Ben (the son of) Yoseph. After his ministry began, he was referred to by his followers as The Messiah (an anointed, consecrated person).

The Euro-gentile Greek interpolators, while attempting to crush rebellion, always sought to prevent the rise of a Messiah in the midst of the Israelites. They inaugurated the process of "name sacrilege". They had been well-taught by their spiritual mentors that men of high, spiritual sensitivity should always pronounce the name of the anointed with profound accuracy. Their first test of "name sacrilege" was initiated with Yeshua the Messiah. They transformed his name, thus successfully transforming his character (in the minds of the people) and amputated his message from its prophetic body. In my book, God the Black Man and Truth ("The Making of a Slave or Soul Transformation" chapter), I explain in greater detail the consequences of being "called out of your name." By calling Yeshua Ben Yoseph Jesus Christ, the Euro-gentiles successfully transformed the spirit of the man and his message to conform to their scheme. How was this accomplished? They gave him a Greek name and then created an image and personality which would be in agreement. Very few people are aware that in spelling and pronunciation, the name "Jesus Christ" is totally Greek. The English derivatives are in harmony with the Greek, not the Hebrew syntax.

11

# LANGUAGE NOTE *(HEBREW)*

Immediately after each word, the English equivalent is written of the correct Hebrew pronunciation.

Next follows the precise pronunciation according to the usual English mode of pronunciation, adapted in such a way that any good Hebraist would immediately recognize the word if so pronounced.

In the case of proper names, we then note the regular mode of Anglicizing it, after the general style of common English.*

**Hebrew**   יֵשׁוּעַ   YESHUA - YAY-SHOO-AH - "JESHUA".
The correct English rendition as a proper
name meaning "He shall save."*

**Hebrew**   מָשִׁיחַ   MAHSHEAHK - MAW-SHEE-AK - The
correct English rendition meaning anointed;
usually a consecrated person (as a king,
priest or saint); anointed, Messiah.*

Thus, the Black African Hebrew Messianic personage was/should be properly called Y(J)ESHUA, Y(J)ESHUA THE MESSIAH, THE MESSIAH or MESSIAH Y(J)ESHUA.

*The Hebrew Greek Key Study Bible - Section: Hebrew and Chaldee Dictionary, pages 5, 52 and 74. Entry numbers 3442 and 4899.

# LANGUAGE NOTE *(GREEK)*

Immediately after each word, the English equivalent is written of the correct Greek pronunciation.

Next follows the precise pronunciation, according to the usual English mode of pronunciation, adapted in such a way that any good Grecist would immediately recognize the word if so pronounced.

In the case of proper names, we then note the regular mode of Anglicizing it, after the general style of common English.*

**Greek** Ιησους    EE-AY-SOOCE - "JESUS" - The English rendition of this proper name. (No meaning given)*

Let us take careful note of the Greek and English similarities in syntax.

Also note that the conspirators dropped the second syllable "ay". The new form gives us Ιησους without the "ay" and with the -I-(EE) becoming the English equivalent - JE - producing the commonly pronounced - JE-SOO-CE. The second syllable - "ay" (η ) was dropped because the pronunciation would have closely resembled the Hebraic name, for example: Y(J)EA SOO (CE). This could have led to Yeshua's name being inadvertently called upon. They preferred to be thorough, preferring an absolute Greek sound in the name.

**Greek** Χριστος    CHRISTOS - KHRIS-TOS; meaning anointed; i.e., the Messiah, an epithet of JESUS - CHRIST.*

*The Hebrew Greek Key Study Bible, - Section: Dictionary of the Greek Testament, pages 5, 37 and 78. Entry numbers 2424 and 5547.

13

We take note that the term is totally Greek in formulation and pronunciation. This word in its Biblical origin was in no way connected with the Hebraic concept of the Messiah or Anointed One.

If the Greek Christos was derived from the Hebrew Mah-she-ahk, the English would render it Messiah, not a proper name, but a title. On the other hand the English translations (Hebrew Canon or Septuagint) for Mah-she-ahk should have consistently remained the **"anointed"** as it was written in the Old Testament, or "Christ" as it was written in the New Testament. This was not the case, for not in one instance in the Old Testament has Mah-she-ahk been translated into English as Christ(os) or Messiah. In conclusion, it is totally incorrect to refer to the Prophetic Messiah as the Christ.

*"And in all things that I have said unto you, be circumspect; and make no mention of the name of other gods, neither let it be heard out of thy mouth."*

**Exodus 23:13**

# Chapter I

# The Rise Of The Messiah: The Myth And The Reality

Imagine, if you will, that a major world war has just ended and thoughts of peace occupy everyone's minds. In the newspaper and on television, words such as "lasting peace" and " an end to all wars" bring comfort to you. A few years pass and complacency sets in. No one considers Armageddon - the war prophesied to bring about the end of this world. As in other generations, everyone shifts Armageddon to a later time and another generation.

Naturally, no one wants to believe that the end of this world will come in his lifetime. Therefore, talk of the end of the world is usually met with scorn or, in some instances, totally ignored because the end of the world means death, destruction and desolation, and no one wants to be a part of that.

But the "war of wars" - or as Saddam Hussein would call it, the "mother of all wars" - will come, causing the disorientation of the entire planet's political, economic and social structure, and holds within it the possibility of destroying 4-1/2 billion of the 5 billion inhabitants of this planet. Is there a solution or salvation?

Any discussion of the end of this world must also incorporate talk of the coming of the Messiah. Many believe that the only Messiah was Jesus, who will return to earth from heaven on a snowy, white cloud surrounded by harp-playing angels with fluffy, white wings. For those of you who feel this image is too outrageous to believe, you are right. Yet, so as not to totally destroy your faith in God and belief that there is a solution and that there will be salvation, it is essential to understand that God, the Almighty Spirit, must be seen through a human face. I want you to have the faith that the Messiah will appear, but do not envision a particular image or person that has been created for you by deceitful interpolators. The established authorities of this world do not plan on relinquishing their power and authority over the people to one opposing everything that these deceitful men have created - without God.

Know of a surety that the end of this world will come in the lifetime of some of you that are reading these words, but in order to be saved from the "abomination of desolation", you must take hold of the Kingdom of God. The Creator has anointed a new Messiah to teach the doctrine of the Kingdom of God, and unfortunately, like the rich ruler who was one of the elite of Yeshua's (Jesus') time, you must be prepared to relinquish your fine homes in lush suburbia, your prestigious jobs and expensive cars.

> *"Now when Jesus heard these things, he said unto him, Yet lackest thou one thing. Sell all that thou hast, and distribute unto the poor, and thou shalt have treasure in heaven; and come, follow me.*
>
> *And when he heard this, he was very sorrowful; for he was very rich.*
>
> *And when Jesus saw that he was very sorrowful, he said, With what difficulty shall they that have riches enter into the kingdom of God!*
>
> *For it is easier for a camel to go through a needle's eye, than for a rich man to enter into the kingdom of God."*
>
> **Luke 18:22-25**

In addition, you must realize that Tom Brokaw will not deliver the news of the coming of the end of the world on the nightly news. If you are to be saved and be a part of the remnant that survives the desolation, then be not like Noah's neighbors who turned their heads and closed their eyes; be not like Moses' challengers who refused to flee Egypt and chose to side with Pharaoh; be not one who Yeshua (Jesus) prayed for that his Father might forgive, "for they [knew] not what they do."

And if you're expecting the Messiah to be a man accompanied by angels wearing wings...well, I hate to disappoint you...

16

## The Messiah and the End of this World

*"And thou shalt become an astonishment, a proverb, and a by-word among all nations to which the Lord shall lead thee."*

**Deuteronomy 28:37**


The multiplicity of curses that befell the Children of Israel was God's way of chastising them because of their trespasses and refusal to be a righteous, model nation which the world could emulate. For the Children of Israel who chose to mimic the heathen, idol-worshipping nation, the ramifications were inevitably ghastly, for God's chastisements were devastating and sure. That erroneous decision not only negatively affected the Children of Israel, but by shirking their Divine charge, they caused all nations and people's dreams of living in a utopian paradise where harmony, justice and love prevailed to be deferred. As it was written,


*"For the earnest expectation of the creation waiteth for the manifestation of the Sons of God. For the creation was made subject to vanity, not willingly, but by reason of him who hath subjected the same in hope. Because the creation itself also shall be delivered from the bondage of corruption into the glorious liberty of the children of God."*

**Romans 8:19-21**


In other words, because the Children of Israel dodged their responsibility to be Godly leaders and pacesetters, and failed to show others the benefit of righteous living, all men were denied the glory of a world where governments were headed by men governed by God. But all is not lost. Therefore, I, Ben Ammi, by the power of the Holy Spirit invested in me, reveal unto the world that there is a Savior nation. Know of a surety that among the people called African Americans, there exists descendants of the ancient Biblical Israelites. The continued suppression of this fact deprives the world of the knowledge of God's redemptive plan for the earth and her wretched inhabitants. It can also be seen as an attempt to cut off or prevent the rise of the Messiah, which is the topic of the following narrative.

17

## The Rise of the Messiah: The Myth and the Reality

To begin with, the word "Messiah" is derived from the Hebrew <u>Mah-she-ahk</u>, meaning "one who anoints". The preferred term used in the gospels is "Christ", which is the shortened version of the Greek word "Christos". In former times, to be anointed by the prophets, priests, kings or men of God carried an air of holiness, as if one had been consecrated to meet or stand before God.

There was a special oil made by the apothecary for the purpose of anointing. (This is not to be mistaken with the mixture used in the service of the Temple which was not to be duplicated. See Exodus 30:22-32.) It was quite common in the days of our Fathers to have one's feet, scalp, and face anointed with a very relaxing oil after a long journey or a day's work in the fields. This was a custom practiced by the Hebrews. Even guests were honored by having their feet and hair oiled. We find that amongst African Americans, the oiling (anointing) of the hair, scalp and face is still very common and relaxing. This custom can be traced back to the ancient Israelite way of life. After an individual's face had been anointed, he would shine and radiate a form of light.

In Hebrew, the same consonants found in the word meaning "a Messianic anointing" were used to describe this radiating process with the use of oil. It was from this process and visual realization that the term Messiah or <u>Mah-she-ahk</u> was developed. The anointed (Messiah or <u>Mah-she-ahk</u>) is one who causes others to shine or radiate light. Thus, we see the definite correlation between this physical undertaking and its spiritual derivative. Thus, the anointed are those upon whom the light had shone.

The apothecary's natural oil made the individual shine and take on an appearance of cleanliness, but more so, of holiness. The Prophet Isaiah alludes to the spiritual counterpart in his words, "Arise and shine, for thy light has come, and the glory of God shall be seen upon you." From these words we may conclude that there is a spiritual similitude that lights up the countenance of men who are exposed to the Truth or Intellect of God. The exposure to God's Truth causes a light to radiate which can be seen in one's way of life and countenance. Therefore, the Messiah (anointed, Savior) is he who has been given the tincture of God's Truth to be used to anoint those that have been on a tedious journey (struggling to live a righteous life in this evil world) and are weary indeed. He will sprinkle the word of God on them that their souls may be refreshed and their strength renewed.

My principal objective is to remove the myth from and return the power to the term "Messiah" ("Christ", in Greek). Furthermore, it is my task to offer clarity in order that those truthfully seeking God (salvation, righteousness, peace of mind, etc.) may find the Deliverer at His advent because His coming may be as a thief in the night. Common sense deems it necessary to know who or what to wait or search for. I feel that this necessity is worth the task.

First, let me call your attention to the origins of the perplexing terminology used concerning the Messiah in many of the translations of the Bible undertaken by those assigned the task by King James.

The Bible has been translated numerous times into many different languages - from Hebrew to Greek, Latin, English, etc. The favorite and most widely-used Bible of the Protestant world is the version of King James, dating back to 1617. King James, just as many other Gentiles, could not resist interposing portions of his own religious interpretations into the deep and profound wisdom of the Holy writings. His ethos demanded that the translations be done in such a way as to fortify his own religious beliefs and be easily adaptable within them. Therefore, he commissioned a group of forty-seven scholars that he personally handpicked and charged them to translate the Hebrew writings. Judging by the mistranslations (as determined by the original meaning and commentary of the Hebrew canon), he obviously had biased input in them.

As is the nature of most autocrats of this period of history, King James' personal viewpoints had to be considered. The translators were forced to take the will and desires of the king into consideration at all times because they dared not displease the king if they cherished their heads. There were endless disputes regarding those translations that were historically recorded. As an illustration, the famous English Minister William Tyndale was persecuted by the leaders of the church because he deviated from the norm of that day - Latin - and translated from the Hebrew and Greek originals.

## The Rise of the Messiah: The Myth and the Reality

Judging from the manner in which the Holy writings were subject to the whims of an egotistical monarch, it is easy to understand how the original Hebrew text of the Bible could be misinterpreted.

When we follow etymologically the path of the word "Christ" (Christos) we find its use very popular among Greek-speaking Hebrews during the second century B. C. E. Crucial to the understanding of someone's usage of the term "Christos," as opposed to "Mahsheahk," is the realization of the thinking of the times. At the time of the advent of Yeshua (Jesus) of Nazareth and at least 100 years prior, to be Hellenized (under Greek cultural influence) was a status symbol. In contemporary history, it probably can be compared to the first Blacks being allowed into white sororities, churches, neighborhoods, places of work, etc. Those who could converse in Greek were considered to be highly learned. Thus, in many circles, there was a preference to use Greek words instead of the more spiritually powerful Hebrew. They felt "Christos" to be a suitable substitute for the Hebrew term Mah-she-ahk, commonly used by the Children of Israel to describe many of their former Kings and used to describe the expectations that the Children of Israel had for a new king. The fact that Israel envisioned a king as a redeemer is well-founded. The term encompassed the individual commission and mission: he was anointed to anoint, to pour out the spirit of God upon the people, to release those bound in darkness (ignorance) and to comfort those that mourn.

In addition, there were certain components of the Hebrew language that were so sensitive that they were not often used in the company of those considered pagan or heretic. One such term was "Messiah" (Mah-she-ahk). To use the term disrespectfully could cause riots and even disruptive rebellion and insurrection amongst the Hebrews. Whereas Yeshua (Jesus) was referred to as the Messiah (Mah-she-ahk) by his followers and many other Israelites, the Roman and Greek hierarchy preferred the term Christos, so as not to offend the sensitive religious sector of Israelites who did not believe in Yeshua (Jesus). For this reason, they attempted to placate the puppets that were subject to them among the Israelites. Their reasoning appears to be tactfully sound. Moreover, their objective for using the term Christos was not motivated by their own religious convictions but by the desire to maintain the political and social order amongst the Hebrews; however, when we see this idiom (Christ) fifteen hundred years later being preferred by those translating from Hebrew and Greek to English, it arouses suspicion of intent. It certainly was not necessary during that era to refer to the "Messiah" as the "Christ", so certainly it should not be used today. During the period when Greece was the ruling power and Hellenization was the "in" thing, the use of the term Christos by the Greek rulers to define the Redeemer was/is understood. Presently, Greece as a ruling power is no more than a note in history. Why, then, is the Greek word "Christ" used to describe the Hebrew Redeemer? Perhaps for the same reasons that the translators left the Hebrew terms Mizraim (Egypt), Cush (Ethiopia), Put (Libya) intact throughout the Bible, so as not to overtly attribute Mizraim, Cush and Put as being the names of African countries, thereby suggesting that all of the great spiritual events that occurred in those countries could be credited to Africa.

Is the consistent use of the word "Christ" motivated by the European community's attempt to perpetuate Euro-gentile (in this case, Greek) cultural and religious influence, while limiting the influence of ancient (African) Hebraic thinking and reasoning? Or could it be an attempt to prevent those searching for Truth and salvation from attaining a clear, lucid understanding of the message and mission of the prophesied Hebrew Messiah? A salient point to remember is that those appointed by King James were imbued with a strong sense of duty to their institutions - not necessarily to the truth. They chose terms that would strengthen their own beliefs and justify their ambitions. Mind you, it was not always a wrong definition substituted, but a word selected that was out of context with the message circumscribed in its scriptural use and/or message.

English is a very deceptive language. Consequently, no other language arouses more concern and suspicion in the areas of Holiness and the True Worship of God. Most spiritual mentors of the Near and Far East, Asia and even those that are circumspect in the Americas prefer spiritual terms in an Asiatic mother tongue or the Holy tongue, Hebrew, rather than English. The Moslem world brings their own Arabic "Allah"; the Hebrews prefer "Yah" or "Ehloheim". Then there are "Jehovah's" Witnesses. Still others prefer carefully selected descriptive phrases such as: The Creator of the Heavens and the Earth, The Almighty, The Most High, etc.

Euro-American/Euro-gentile language is never used to pronounce the sacred name of the Most High and when the language is used as a medium of communication, the thought has to be of a language that is more in spiritual harmony with the message and messengers of God. The Masters who have been chosen by the Almighty must, in some instances, walk a linguistic tightrope while providing the light to guide humanity back unto God.

Let us take a point of reference from the contemporary use of English by the African American. The former chattel slave, while adopting the former slavemaster's language as his own, has not succeeded in altering the Englishman's concept of his own language nor his power to define the meanings that have been derived from his historical, cultural and social experience. For example, the African American takes great pride in being referred to as "Black" American, whereas the Euro-American/Euro-gentile explains the same term Black (pigmentation) as a curse and disgrace, because the so-called progenitor of the Black race, Ham, was supposedly cursed Black[1] according to the Euro-gentile interpolators of the Bible. This curse exists unto this day wherever Blacks may be found upon this planet.

No matter how vociferous or comprehensive the African American's explanation of Blackness, the original meaning given by the Englishman has prevailed. The Euro-gentile does not attempt to prevent Blacks' use of the term; he thinks it pacifies them. He, as a matter of fact, is pleased in knowing that everyone seeking an authoritative definition of what is being perpetrated by their use of the term will inevitably know and accept what was meant when he formulated the words used to describe Black pigmentation.[2] The only recourse for the African American would be to select other, more suitable terminology, or select the definition of Black from an African language that coincides with his inner feelings and insist that the English Language Institute of America insert this definition and a note concerning the language from which it

[1] See <u>God the Black Man and Truth</u>, page 23.

[2] See <u>God the Black Man and Truth</u>, page 143.

was derived. This is common practice for words whose meanings are associated with other languages such as Greek, French, German, etc. Other than that, he should accept as a temporary substitute the term "African American".

When I elucidate, I relate to the Hebrew thought to offer you clarity and spiritual assistance in your selection and use of terminology. This, with the blessings of the Holy One of Israel, is merely to allow you to select the term more suitable and compatible to express your message so that you are not easily deceived. In some instances you may find it necessary to slightly alter or change your commonly used vocabulary for a better selection of words more spiritually conducive to your relationship to the Creator God. Remember always that the struggle against the sons of darkness, or those who do not desire for you to see the light, is a confrontation between the lie and the truth, deception versus clarity.

In continuing my exegesis, I must emphasize another outstanding point. No matter how a Greek individual might say Christos ("Christ"), it can never compare to a Hebrew saying Mah-she-ahk, ("Messiah"). The two concepts behind the formulation and the use of the terms greatly differ. Closer investigation of the etymological meaning of each would undoubtedly reveal that difference, while the spirituality of each word transcends the corporeal and delves deeper into the subconscious, revealing greater variations of thought. I've reached this conclusion for several reasons. One is that at Yeshua's (Jesus') advent, the Hebrews and the Greeks were worlds apart in their concept of God. The Hebrews were monotheistic and the Greeks were polytheistic. During the time of Yeshua (Jesus), heathenism was the common practice of all the nations surrounding Israel, inclusive of Greece. So when a Hebrew called upon his God, and a Grecian his god, it was not the same. The obeisance paid to various dieties by Grecians had to differ to a greater or lesser degree, whereas the one God of the Hebrews received all of their reverence, at least from those that adhered to the faith. So when a Hebrew says Mah-she-ahk ("Messiah"), and a Grecian says Christos ("Christ"), there is a definite difference.

Trying to use a Greek term without knowing the Greek definition of the term or underlying motive for using such a term is absurd. In translating the words, we must also attempt to translate the thought behind the words being used. This gives us greater clarity of the message to be derived from the messenger. What I am saying is that through the subtle use of language, the Euro-American/Euro-gentile has cut off the African American and others from most of the true knowledge of the African Hebrew Messianic figure who lived and taught approximately two thousand years ago. His name in Hebrew was Ye-shu-a, who was called the Mah-she-ahk. In Greek, he was called Jesous Christos. If the Greek was an accurate form of the Hebrew, then the English would render his name: Y(J)eshua the Messiah. Instead, the popular use is the intentional mistranslation Jesus Christ, which is the English form of the Greek - not the Hebrew - completely amputating the personage and his true message from the unsuspecting populace.

Thus, we can safely and accurately draw our conclusion: if the Greek Jesous Christos was an accurate renaming of the Hebrew Ye-shu-a, who was called the Mah-she-ahk, the English derivative would have him being called Yeshua the Messiah. But since it doesn't, it arouses deep suspicion of both the Greek and English thought behind the term being used. Since we are certainly aware that the objective of those under the satanic spirit of err is to deceive, we certainly must ask ourselves if there is deep-seated deception involved in our religious practices which have led our people astray from God. Again, deception is defined as: to be led astray; to cause to accept as true or valid what is false or invalid (Webster's New Collegiate Dictionary, 1981). It is no small matter that our Christian brothers were not taught to shout out "Messiah Yeshua", "Yeshua the Messiah", "I thank you Yeshua", or "just have faith in the Lord Yeshua". This would have kept them in the arena of Truth, hope and reality. At the least, it would have kept them in touch somewhat with a God that could help them, the God of their fathers - the Almighty, Holy One of Israel.

If there was no difference then, it was vanity for God to vary the languages as He did when He baffled the builders of the Tower of Babel. Moreover, Hebrew is the Holy tongue, to be spoken by or used by Holy people to render a Holy result or a by-product which will be pleasing unto God.

Let us further consider: why is it that in not one instance in the Old Testament where the word Mah-she-ahk (Messiah) is used in the

Hebrew text has the word Messiah been written, or for that matter, the gospel-preferred Greek word Christ? Why was it that in every instance the less accurate word "anointed" was selected even in instances where it was grammatically incorrect as is the case in Psalms 105:6-15, where in Hebrew it is used in the plural tense, referring to the Children of Israel, and not in the singular? (These verses give the narrative total clarity, while the 15th verse holds the definite point being referred to.) On the other hand, when translating the gospels and epistles, the Greek term "Christ" was left in the text instead of the English derivatives, "Messiah" or "anointed".

Let us now walk in the light of God's Truth. Consider Samuel's words while standing before Eliab: "Surely the Lord's Messiah is before him". Imagine David calling Saul "God's Messiah". Then there was David being called "the Messiah of God", from whom was established a Messianic throne and thus he that would inherit the throne of David would be called Messiah. (The Messiah spoken of by the Prophet Isaiah [Isaiah 9:6-7] was to sit on the throne of David.) After that event, God would refer to the upright Nation of Israel as His Messiahs. Then, upon our introduction to the gospels and hearing Yeshua (Jesus) being referred to as "Yeshua the Messiah", we would be much clearer in our honest and authentic expectations. Our minds and thoughts would automatically reflect back to the books of the Hebraic canon. We would have a more thorough and lucid understanding of the Messiah's mission and even why it is necessary that He be ordained. It is just the opposite when we hear "Jesus the Christ". The Greek word Christos limits our understanding and directs us away from the roots from which Yeshua the Messiah sprang forth. It clouds his calling and his mission, and worst of all, it points our minds and thoughts in the direction of Europe. And Europe keeps us looking to the sky and to the "sweet by and by". It was Europe that invented the celebration of the 25th day of December as the birth of "Jesus the Christ". And as an added attraction to that famous date, they attached "Santa Claus". Moreover, Europe produced Easter as the day of "Christ's" resurrection and celebrated it by giving gifts of colorful eggs laid by the "Easter Bunny". What I am alluding to is that these things have been done intentionally to prohibit the earth's afflicted peoples from achieving salvation - to hedge up the way with thorns that they not find their way back unto God.

## The Rise of the Messiah: The Myth and the Reality

God has commanded all of the families of man to come forth and acknowledge His law of life that they may live. But the generations of the Euro-gentiles despise the Most High God and refuse to accept His established order. An evil seed has been sown and the fruit thereof is abundant. And the hour is at hand during which the sowers must inevitably reap their harvest. Their imaginations are vain and their glory deceitful by which they themselves are deluded. The infallible Word of God has determined that the web they weaved for others has ensnared them.

Let us go for a point of reference to the book of St. John 4:25,26, 28-29, 42. It is in this chapter that Yeshua (Jesus) meets and converses with the Samaritan woman at the well. It is of utmost importance that we make careful note of some very significant points in the dialogue. Thus: "The woman said unto Him I know that the Messiah shall come [Mah-she-ahk is written in the Hebrew scriptures] which is called Christos. When he cometh, he will tell us all things." The object here is the use of the word Messiah, which the Greeks, Romans or foreigners call "The Christos" (Christ), a secondary term. Yeshua (Jesus) responds, "I that spake unto you am He (the Messiah)". It does not require much imagination to know that He replied by referring to himself as the Messiah and not as Christ. The two words being used here in close proximity allow us to conclude that the term "Christos" is not a direct translation of the Hebrew "Mah-she-ahk" but merely a Greek alternative derived from a totally Greek concept of a messenger of a god. Therefore, in other places where we see the Mah-she-ahk (Messiah) being referred to as Christos (Christ), we must remember the term is merely a Greek substitute and not an accurate translation. You must keep in mind that Yeshua (Jesus) was a man of God and highly spiritual and sensitive to the innermost feelings of the poor and needy. There is no way to conclude that He would have preached the Kingdom of Heaven to His people using the language of their oppressor. Two thousand years ago the Greeks and Romans were the pagan subjugators of the African Hebrews. Yeshua (Jesus) would not have referred to Himself as the Greek "Christos". A review of the social condition at that time would give credence to this conclusion.

When the woman testified before the men of the city, she said: "Come, and see a man, which told me all things that ever I did. Is not this the Christ?" The problem here is that from verse 23 we know she had previously heard the word Christ, but she did not use this idiom when testifying before the men of the city. She said, "Is not this the Messiah (Mah-she-ahk)?" We are keen to note that four verses earlier the translator knew the difference between Messiah and Christ or Mah-she-ahk and Christos. That being the absolute Truth, why did they conspire to mistranslate the women's words: "Is not this the Messiah?" Further on we find the same "oversight" in verse 42: "We have heard him ourselves, and know that this is indeed the Christ, the Savior of the World." Again, the Greek word Christ was used instead of Messiah as it is written in the Hebrew text.

We should also take note that in verse 42, the laymen testify that the actions of the Hebrew Messiah would have a positive influence on the lives of men throughout the world. Subsequently, there was no need to alter his character or historical record regarding His Hebraic origin or lifestyle.

Truth was not created to deride anyone's religious beliefs. Those that hold fast to a lie deride themselves. Truth is meant to shine a light on the path for all men, regardless of their convictions. It comes to help and not to hinder men in their search for God and His magnificent plan of salvation. The worst position that a man of God could take would be one that makes him comfortable believing a lie.

With God, there has to be order with all things. There is a definite order established for the Plan of Redemption for the House of Israel and all humanity. Included in God's Plan of Redemption is the essentiality of two distinct Messiahs. First, there is a Messiah or a Messianic individual and second, there is a Messianic people. The Messianic individual is always at center stage. For it is he that has the anointing oil (Truth-doctrine of salvation - light of God). He alone is the primary mediator between the people and God. Not only is his job to anoint the Messianic people but when they go astray, it is his responsibility to regather them. He is the suffering servant that has to preach salvation unto the lost or confused Messianic people and return them to their "calling" in God. This is usually done in the midst of much opposition and rebellion, not to mention the necessity of overcoming the impediments and problems implanted by the adversaries of God. Remember I said earlier in this chapter that amongst the African Americans are descendants of the ancient Biblical Israelites, the Children of Israel or in other words, the Messianic people. The Messiah has to nevertheless bear their iniquities and abuse. When Yeshua (Jesus) said, "I am the Messiah", I'm sure he knew well the character and role of the savior.

The Messianic individual has to be empowered by God, for it is He that will provide his comfort on a lonely and often inglorious path. The prophets of God give a very detailed description of the Messiah's life after the fall of the Messianic people. Under the influence of their oppressors, they became stiff-necked and rebellious; they killed the prophets and stoned the messengers of God who were sent unto them.

A similar scenario presently exists in the midst of African Americans. They, too, have become content with impotent leadership and an apathetic existence. Deranged minds, myopic vision and dull ears are prevalent - all valid and accurate characteristics used to describe them. They have been completely westernized - culturally, religiously, spiritually and physically. Their religious leaders appear to be tranquilized with the religious dogma granted them by their present oppressors, the children of the enslavers of our forefathers. It is perplexing but factual that the former slavemaster has been transformed into the savior, an incredible paradox.

The Messiah is called the suffering servant of God because he is chosen to lay bare the evils hidden under the carpet by preaching the Truth, forcing you to consider things you've been trying to ignore. He is resisted instead of assisted, abased not praised, threatened not encouraged, misrepresented instead of given credibility. When the revelation of Truth comes, it does not lead many to seek repentance and forgiveness, but causes discomfort with the messenger's presence and the desire for the revealer to be removed or destroyed. Understandably, true messengers of God will find it hard to get a hearing in this world. Every sincere messenger of God should be prepared to have his character assassinated by satan's hidden "teachers of righteousness". And if that doesn't work, attempted physical destruction is imminent.

Consider Amos, the Prophet of God, when Amaziah, the priest ( the clergy) who should have recognized and supported him, told him to get out and not to come back. (Amos 7:12) The adversaries of God neither go in themselves neither will they allow those that desire to do so to go therein. Theirs shall be the greater damnation. They shall in no wise escape the judgment of God. They oppose righteousness because they have become an integral part of the Euro-American/Euro-gentile society. The anointed of God have lifted these societies into the light of God and found them to be rotten.

These words are a disturbing message, like a strong wind blowing through the slums of the cities as well as the countrysides, causing fallout and shock waves. The shepherds of my people have led them astray and received the trappings of success in exchange for the sacrificing of their souls. The teaching of Truth in this evil world is a very hazardous occupation, as it reveals the degenerate heart of man and the delight he has in walking contrary to the laws of God. These revelations of man's sordid state of existence, specifically that of the African American, should be seen as a magnanimous effort to cause him to cry out for mercy, forgiveness and cleansing. View my words not as a mere condemnation, but as my preference that you live by accepting God's plan of salvation for your wretched soul. Initially, you need only to cry out unto the Holy One of Israel; He is aware that you need help to overcome the multiplicity of evil impediments placed before you. This is why He always sends a savior to guide you to the fountain of living waters to be cleansed. When you cry out unto God and confess that you are ready to meet His conditions, a covenant is made. The Deliverer then moves you through the purification process which will bring your life back into harmony with your Heavenly Father.

Just as it was in the days of old as years passed and oppression increased from without and within, the moans and groans of the Holy people caused God to send them Moses - the Redeemer, Messiah - to deliver them out of Egyptian bondage. Once again, a little light was manifested in the minds of a small group of African Hebrew men, women and children that had become disgusted with the wiles of the evil society and treacherous leadership; subsequently, they sought the assistance of the Holy One of Israel, the Creator God. God had promised that at any time and from any place, He would be found of them if they would seek Him with all sincerity. This was promised through Moses and confirmed in Solomon's prayer and in the words of the Prophets.

Why had the people prayed unto God for a Messiah or Deliverer? They had leaders and judges and religious mentors. That, no doubt, was part of the problem; the inept leaders had exhibited hypocrisy, inequity exploitation and abuse in their positions of influence over them, greatly influencing the peoples' cries unto God. What kind of leadership did they expect from a Messiah? The absolute! They wanted someone who would come and take complete control of their lives with the authority and help of God. This is the essence of a Messiah. He is sent by God with absolute authority to take control over the destiny of the people. For the Children of Israel, it meant that they be returned unto God, the Law, their Messianic calling and responsibility to the nations of the earth. The priority of the Messianic nation is to show forth the Glory of God in their lifestyles and morality, that they may bear witness to the benefit of a people living under the laws (instructions) of God. The conspirators were also aware that the people were to pattern themselves in the image of the Messiah. To offset this, they developed the cliche "Christ-like". Yet, despite appearances, few people fully and truthfully understand the significance of this popular contemporary Christian term.

Once again profound deception prevails; people are confused because there is no clear, lucid understanding. Yet, the conspirators (those whose authority would be compromised by the Messiah's coming) knew the term "Christ-like" would soothe the followers of the newly-founded religion. They then needed only to create the desired character for the Christos they had introduced, thereby causing the people to become molded in the new personality, and actually adopting an image in complete opposition to the true image of the African Hebrew Messiah; again, a very devious scheme to cut off the Truth and true Messiah from the world. Yet, all things done in darkness must come to light. The ultimate purpose of the scheme had to eventually be revealed. We began with name sacrilege, from which was conceived a false direction, a false purpose, a false religion. And a false image is now decorating the walls of your homes, the interior of your chapels and churches. A complete transformation has taken place, leaving neither a mental nor physical resemblance of the ancient Black African Hebrew Messiah, Yeshua.

In the beginning it was the word (the name) and the wrong name was brought forth by the adversary of God. It was the beginning and through it all these other things were fashioned and made.

"The beginning of every substance is thought. Before substance can be manifested there must be thought. Thought is spirit, the unseen, but it does not remain unseen. The thoughts of a man are soon revealed in the substance of deeds which follow those thoughts.

The Euro-gentile gave you the idea of an inferiority complex in your early childhood, even before you could read. Children receive their first worldly images and impressions from pictures. Therefore, before you could read, you opened the Bible, and from the pictures you received your first impression of God and angels, and you have never forgotten what you saw. You saw pictures of a European Jesus on the cross, a European Jesus carrying the cross, and teaching the people on the Mount of Olives. You saw a picture of a European, Mary, the mother of Jesus, and you saw pictures of angels in negligees with wings on their backs. You saw many other pictures of Europeans being cast in the surroundings of the Holy Land. As you grew up, you never realized that it was those childhood thoughts of Euro-gentiles as God that started you on the path of attempting to prove yourself worthy and acceptable to Europeans. He has portrayed himself as God having both your future and your destiny in his hands.

They kept those pictures (thoughts) before you all of your life, everywhere you went, in every store, in every home, and on almost every wall of your church. Now you even feel offended when someone suggests that the pictures be taken down and destroyed. When someone mentions the racist connotation of these pictures to European Christians or others, the favorite answer is "God doesn't have any color." And, worse yet, he turns around and implies that the one who raises the question is a racist.

Why is it that the problem of race only enters the picture when we begin discussing positive Black images? How could it be that all of these artists have had such a vivid imagination of all those characters

31

being European, but none of them have ever imagined that those African Hebrews in that African land (Israel) were Black?"

God the Black Man and Truth

It is the nature of the race problem within the European world that precludes true social, political and economic equality and justice through amalgamation. They are not prepared to accept their own true history. Certainly that negates their acceptance of our true history. He cannot accept us until he is ready to accept Truth. He cannot accept Truth when his greatness is founded upon a lie; to tell or accept Truth would shake the very rudiments of the Euro-American/Euro-gentile world. Therefore, Truth is a threat to that which is giving him so much satisfaction. Thus, the primary problem is not our Black skin, but the Truth, which is the companion of our Black pigmentation. If he could dissect us from Truth, he would have less of a problem accepting our complexion. He tried this method and he wasn't successful. First, he failed in his attempt to destroy knowledgeable slaves and elders, then through deceptive education. The primary reason for his failure is that Truth is tied directly into the existence of the Eternal. It is He that has to prevent the destruction of Truth. Therefore, it is the exposure of himself, his women, his children, and social nature to Truth which the Euro-gentile is warring against. He has no problem accepting Hebraic philosophical concepts. He can even accept a "non-consanguineous" Hebrew savior created in his image and likeness. His problem is strictly his own personal egocentric race problem. It is for that reason that he alone has attempted to transform the Egyptians, Ethiopians, the Hebrews and all of the highly developed ancient world from Black to white. He has authorized book burnings, destruction of manuscripts and interpolation, in his vain attempt to destroy the roots and origins he was born from, trying to conceal all evidence of the fact that in the beginning all people were "colored" - brown or black pigmented. In other words, the Euro-gentiles fear the revelation of their true Black father and mother. Evidence supporting the fact that the first man was black pigmented has been obscured - hidden - in order to keep any significant credit or accolades to this effect being attributed to the Black race; the deception is severely deep-rooted.

For example, has it ever occurred to you just how the 12 lost tribes of Israel got lost? Why is it that man can put a man on the moon, cause the clouds to rain, and travel at the speed of light, but no one knows the true history of the African American? But the Truth is coming to light. The race problem is the making of the European world and has trapped him on a dead end street.

I have no race problem; neither do the great majority of African people. We are patient, for our Father has assured us that no lie is forever; only Truth can live and thus cause man to live forever. At this time in history, the universal forces have come forth demanding Truth as the price that has to be paid for immortality. Everlasting damnation awaits all of those who oppose the exaltation of Truth. This is the final call to Euro-gentiles and their adherents. Judgment Day has come; remove the leavening from your hearts and homes; cast away the garments of lies and deception that I may sprinkle clean water upon you that you may be brought pristine before the throne of the Holy One of Israel, the one Creator God. He will clothe you with Truth everlasting that we may go hand in hand as one, uprooting the lies and propagating the Truth. This Truth will free you and open your eyes to comprehend the difference between the Hebraic and Greek concepts of deification. You will cross over from the path called "Christ-like" to the Messianic path. You will see clearly that you were to be in the image of the Messiah and in his likeness. This meant that upon his acceptance as your savior, you became Messiah-like or Messianic. Your return to proper terminology will greatly assist you in finding your true purpose and calling which can only be revealed to you by the Messiah.

To be Messianic brings clarity to your mission and his. To be fashioned in the image and likeness of the Messiah would have given you a moral responsibility to the nations, for to be Yeshua-like or like Yeshua was to be Messianic.

Men have not been able to measure or determine the benefit of a righteous lifestyle both physically and mentally, because those chosen to proclaim the glory of righteousness had turned aside. In the interim, no other people or nation has risen, or been sufficiently motivated by a quest for righteousness, to take their place. What will be the results of a society of true brotherhood, sisterhood, familyhood and childhood?

There will be no drugs or perversion. You will hear Godly music, see Divine theatre and dance, witness no stealing, exploitation or murder, or feel worry or oppression. In addition, in these the days of the Kingdom of God, the Truth of God will guide humanity back to the realization that morality and the application of righteous principles and procedures will solve the majority of man's biological problems.

*"Be not wise in thine own eyes; fear the Lord, and depart from evil.*

*It shall be health to thy navel, and marrow to thy bones."*

**Proverbs 3:7-8**

*"My son, attend to my words; incline thine ear unto my sayings,*

*Let them not depart from thine eyes; keep them in the midst of thine heart.*

*For they are life unto those that find them, and health to all their flesh.*

*Keep thy heart with all diligence; for out of it are the issues of life."*

**Proverbs 4:20-23**

*"The fear of the Lord prolongeth days, but the years of the wicked shall be shortened."*

**Proverbs 10:27**

*"A sound heart is the life of the flesh; but envy, the rottenness of the bones."*

**Proverbs 14:30**

*"A merry heart doeth good like a medicine, but a broken spirit drieth the bones."*

**Proverbs 17:22**

In the aforementioned Biblical references we receive our sacred reminder that physiology is definitely influenced by the spirit of man. There is/was a living organism in man that is activated by righteous behavior as has been determined by God Almighty. Without proper mannerisms and a Godly character which yields the proper chemistry that causes certain cells, organs and tissues to function, death is inevitable. Just as there are proper nutritional requirements for man's body, there are spiritual requirements for his soul. Without the sacred secretions caused by the right interaction with fellowman and God, many vital organs will either die or at the least, start the process of perpetual decay.

The Word of God informs us that the process of life, living and good health depend on more than wholesome food, "for man does not live by bread alone," but also by a way of life that is prescribed by God. Only if a man can hear, accept and activate Truth will he receive the strength to revitalize the organism whose function is dependent solely on a proper spiritual diet. When these organs come alive they allow man to enter the realm of immortality. The carnal Euro-gentile knowledge of medicine does not even enter into this realm, nor does the Euro-gentile understand that God has connected good health with good behavior. Yet, even his doctors have been forced to acknowledge that depression and anxiety have a very negative effect on the health of man.

To broaden this perspective, I must add that evil in its entirety is a contagious disease. The chaos of Euro-gentile theological concepts inhibits men's understanding and impedes their struggle against the forces of evil, and blinds them from acknowledging that the struggle is universal - not individual. It teaches men to seek only personal peace for their salvation as if an evil environment will have no effect upon them. This attitude fortifies evil, perpetuating its existence, preventing its extinction, and will ultimately overcome the individualist. Whereas when the Sons of Light are vigilant in their pursuit of Godliness, evil is never comfortable anywhere on this planet. They are not satisfied with an evil-free home in a city, state and country engulfed in wickedness. Iniquitous and evil works affect the well-being of people outside of the immediate boundary of execution. For example, evil rulers or politicians affect the rest, sleep and peaceful meditations of the Sons of Light wherever they are, for we are affected by the suffering and destruction that they cause our fellowman. We are our brother's keeper.

## The Rise of the Messiah: The Myth and the Reality

All men in opposition to God must know that even if their geographical location is far in distance from the Sons of Light, the Sons are active on behalf of the adversaries' victims. Truth has no peaceful habitation in the midst of lies. Again I note: the spread of AIDS is affecting the physiology of all people on this planet. The anxiety alone is taking a heavy toll on years of life from people, even in an AIDS - free environment. The forces of evil cannot be allowed a feeling of comfort any place on this earth. True - we, the Sons of Light, seek inner peace, yet we understand that we are an organ of a human family; therefore, an enemy of that family is our enemy. The Messianic nation has to share the God intellect, display its positive effects and encourage all men to join hands in the Universal struggle against the forces of evil. Together we shall soon put an end to the arrogance of the proud and abase the haughtiness of the ruthless. The two Messiahs - the anointed individual and the chosen people - are united in purpose and mission. Indeed, it's a mythical concept to think that the Messiah will personally visit all the nations in order to evangelize the doctrine of the Kingdom of God, yet his teachings, will be disseminated unto the world by way of the Messianic nation. The Messiah is commissioned to resurrect (in this case) the lost sheep of the House of Israel and guide them in the application of his teachings, that they in turn become God's light unto the nations. That is not to say that the Messiah is a hypothetical prototype of man. He is a real, tangible person and many people will in fact see, touch and speak with him. He will personally, as well as spiritually, affect a positive change in the lives of multitudes. The doctrine that he bestows upon the Messianic people will be universal and he will share it with many. Nevertheless, he is cognizant of the process of redemption as handed down by God to His inspired messengers, the prophets. Only within this harmonious realm can the Word of God be activated; therefore, the prophets charged the Messiah to begin his mission in the midst of his people - The Hebrews - the incapacitated Messianic nation.

*"These twelve Jesus sent forth, and commanded them, saying, Go not into the way of the Gentiles, and into any city of the Samaritans enter not;*

*But go, rather, to the lost sheep of the house of Israel."*

**St. Matthew 10:5-6**

*"And because He said, I was not sent except to the lost sheep of the House of Israel.*

*She came and bowed down to him saying, my Lord, help me.*

*And he replied saying, it is not good to take the children's bread and cast it to the young of dogs.*

*And she said, correct my Lord, however, also the young of dogs shall eat crumbs that fall from on the table of the Lord."*

**St. Matthew 15:24-27**


*"Ye are the salt of the earth, but if the salt have lost its savor, with what shall it be salted? It is thereafter good for nothing, but to be cast out, and to be trodden under foot of men.*

*Ye are the light of the world. A city that is set on a hill cannot be hidden.*

*Neither do men light a lamp, and put it under a bushel, but on a lampstand, and it giveth light unto all that are in the house.*

*Let your light so shine before men, that they may see your good works, and glorify your Father, who is in heaven."*

**St. Matthew 5:13-16**


The aforementioned scriptural references edify the Messianic path of Yeshua (Jesus) of Nazareth. I feel it necessary to again remind you that Yeshua's (Jesus') entire ministry was based around his acceptance of the prophetic vision for his people and the world. We find Yeshua (Jesus) instructing his Apostles to take his teachings to the House of Israel - a prerequisite of spreading the doctrine of salvation unto all nations.

The Sermon on the Mount was taught with upward of 95% of the participants being Israelites. He recognized them as having a special mission amongst the earth's inhabitants. He spoke unto them on this wise: "Ye are the light of the world;" that is, "Your way of life should give light that all men may see and glorify the Heavenly Father." They were not chosen because they were preponderant amongst all of the nations, but because of His love for the Israelites and merciful concern for the nations. The Messianic people are therefore warned not to be puffed up or highminded, but to fear because their calling is of God, not of man.

Historically, we find Muhammad and other saviors of similar understanding contemplating their relationship to God's plan and their people. Muhammad as the Mahdi did not see himself as the immediate savior of the world beyond his Arabian nation. He was sent to them to teach, instruct and commission them with the moral responsibility of sharing salvation with all men. Therefore, the coming of the Mahdi would first impact on the nations of Islam to revive their sense of responsibility to the human family, and the first testimonies of his coming would inevitably proceed from a Moslem, not a Christian or Hebrew. That brings us face to face with another major obstacle which, in former times, was insurmountable... his acceptance.

Why would this be such an obstruction? As a result of the diversity of religious dogma, men's minds have been disoriented. Consequently, they have been subtly indoctrinated to expect some extraordinary phenomenon which will not appear (such as a winged beast or some other type of preposterous person or thing). So when the Messiah or Deliverer comes, his coming will be disapproved of, excessively questioned and ultimately rejected by many. The magnitude of the deception that has been perpetrated upon man, coupled with the essential requirement that he make a positive change, shall block man's acceptance of the Messiah. This is mere truth; there is no way that the Messiah could prove his authenticity to them. They will ostracize him and cast him out. The scenario could very well be the Messiah and Jerusalem versus the Pope and the Vatican; the powerless versus the powerful; the poor and the needy - versus those in control of the earth's resources and wealth; the arms of militarism, ideological propaganda and intrigue (overt and covert government-sponsored operations against both nature and people) versus the armour of God: truth, love of God, nature and fellowman.

One of the primary objectives of a Deliverer is to save the people from convictions and false beliefs that are killing them. You must, of your own choice, come out of this world, for it is written: "the prince of this world is satan." There shall come a time when no man shall be able to make intercession for or save those that have held/hold fast to iniquity, or on the other hand, oppress those that have overcome this evil world. To do what is good shall bring forth power; in contrast, wickedness causes weakness.

At this point we should also take note that the initial motif of the Epistles concerning the Messianic message of Yeshua (Jesus) was, in most cases, in harmony with the words of the prophets. The thrust of their message was that the salvation of the Messianic nation could only be accomplished through the acceptance of the Messiah or Deliver sent by God. His presence would supersede all religious and social authority. To illustrate this point, consider how the Black church wields tremendous power over the Black community. However, it is essential to understand that the authority of the Messiah supersedes the power of the church. Any attempt by the church body to attain their elevation or salvation by other means was/is destined to failure. Yeshua (Jesus) said: "He that entereth not by the door into the sheepfold, but climbeth up some other way, the same is a thief and a robber." Again, it is imperative for lay persons and mentors to study the words of the prophets before passing on the opinions of the Epistles. Anyone attempting to formulate an opinion otherwise will be confused and will thereby only confuse others.

Historically, we find that the House of Israel had been very hostile and churlish toward those sent by God unto them. We find Ezekiel the Prophet skeptical and afraid to go to the rebellious House of Israel. In addition, Yeshua (Jesus) solidified this fact by stating (while lamenting over their blindness):

*"O Jerusalem, Jerusalem, thou that killest the prophets, and stonest them who are sent unto thee, how often would I have gathered thy children together, even as a hen gathereth her chickens under her wings, and ye would not!*

*Behold, your house is left unto you desolate.*

*For I say unto you, Ye shall not see me henceforth, till ye shall say, Blessed is he that cometh in the name of the Lord."*

**St. Matthew 23:37-39**

*"Why will ye plead with me? Ye all have transgressed against me, saith the Lord.*

*In vain have I smitten your children; they received no correction. Your own sword hath devoured your prophets, like a destroying lion."*

**Jeremiah 2:29-30**

. . . telling the people that they would not witness the presence of God in their midst until they blessed the one who was sent in His name. Therefore, when we understand the prophetic, Messianic message, many things attributed to Yeshua (Jesus) can be seen in their proper perspective. The inquiries concerning Yeshua's (Jesus') calling and authority were coming from two camps: those hoping that he was the messenger and those hoping that he was not. The laymen were trying to prove that he was and the religious authorities were challenged to prove that he was not. The entire scenario was him coming to save the Messianic people in the midst of much hypocrisy, clamor and confusion.

We find Peter in a similar situation. Peter had been ordered to come before the religious authorities because he was one of Yeshua's (Jesus') disciples and after Yeshua was crucified, his followers were also sought out by the authorities. He stated to those who had plotted against him and unto all Israel: "Neither is there salvation in any other for there is no other name under heaven given among men, whereby we must be saved." He was a believer who was attempting to make those purporting to be of God understand that they had greatly erred by rejecting the Messiah. He was not trying to convince the world but only those who refused to relinquish to their successor, the Messiah, their control and authority over the people. Peter also stated there is no other name given. But did he really mean a literal name or did he mean a spirit? If he meant a literal name then what name did he use? He certainly did not use Jesous Christos, which is the Greek alternative for the Hebrew name Yeshua Mah-she-ahk, which means Messianic Savior. If we sincerely feel that there is power in his name, then we would better understand why his name was mistranslated. That could very well be why the preference was for the pagan Greek language instead of the Holy tongue Hebrew. Those that understand the power of words must also consider the deception of words. Many people are referring to a "Jesus Christ" while in actuality, there was no Savior referring to himself by that name.

I will again return to the Prophet Isaiah for light on this subject. Isaiah said a child would be born and his name would be called Emanuel, which in Hebrew means "God is with us." If that was to be taken literally, Mary and Joseph would have called their son Emanuel as prescribed by the Prophet and the angel. But they didn't. The key, then, becomes the spiritual significance of "God is with us." God's message unto us concerning this is thus: when the word of God comes alive in spirit or in the flesh of His messengers, it is God in the midst of the people. This is not to be limited to one individual, but a continuous line of individuals sent by God; e.g., Noah, Moses, Abraham.

This lineage began before the fall of Adam and has continued on to this day. The names of God's chosen messengers - the Messiahs, whose calling is to deliver the people of God - have been different but their calling the same. They were "God" within the Messianic nation. In other words, as was written in Exodus 7:1: "And the Lord said unto Moses, see, I have made thee a god. . ."; also in Psalms 82:6: "I have said ye are gods. . ." Yeshua (Jesus) said: "Before Abraham was, I am." He meant that God's anointed messenger was Emanuel, representing God in the midst of the people. Remember, Yeshua (Jesus) said that John the Baptist was Elijah who was prophesied to come. (St. Matthew 11:13-15) But his name was not Elijah (which in Hebrew means "My God is Yah"). If John could be called Elijah, then we know that it was his Godly spirit that deemed he be called Elijah, not necessarily that he was named Elijah. If John could be Elijah, then someone else could be Yeshua (Jesus, the Savior) and not be called Yeshua (Jesus). If that is true, then someone else could have already been Yeshua (Jesus) prior to his advent, even though being called by a different name.

Yeshua (Jesus) said the same words I am saying: it is the spirit that quickeneth; the flesh profits nothing. The Euro-gentile has formulated a doctrine of religious deception to prevent the attainment of salvation and to dissuade men from the true quest for God. Christianization is/was a means to Europeanize the world and used to ease opposition to Western civilization. They have created a mass of traditions and interpretations, and superimposed them as the Laws of God. Appearing as an interpreter of God's laws, satan, disguised as religious or evangelistic, has interpolated the laws of God and camouflaged them within the doctrine of contemporary religionists talking about Jesus returning while giving the deceptive impression that he will be welcomed. In the same manner, the religionists of two thousand years ago were waiting for the Messiah.

Religion headed up by Euro-gentiles has been tactfully structured to deceive the Messianic nation and all of the earth's inhabitants into rejecting the Savior and salvation. It stands to reason that his religion is designed to deceive you. God's truth and salvation must ultimately save you from him. We must always keep in mind when reading the Euro-gentile's dissertations and prognostications concerning the end of this (his) world: they are not motivated by God nor by the desire to reveal Truth. It is in this same regard that they use the Bible. Their objectives have caused them to misdirect the people concerning the prophecies. This does not destroy the authenticity of the Word of God but men of God's spirit must properly interpret the Word of God in order to fulfill God's will. In every nation under the sun the criteria will be the same: fear God and do what is right as prescribed by Him. As God moves His spirit upon me, causing me to teach you Truth, I admonish you to be wise. Receive it as potentially great wealth and use it to improve your relationship with God. If you take these truths and invest them into your soul, the bank of life, you shall be greatly rewarded. To invest them properly requires that you have faith in them. Afterwards, they will work for you year after year. No other investment you've ever made will return so much in life. If you do not invest these truths, you will lose the opportunity and the promised dividend because of your slothful misbelief. The affluence gained from your investment will cause you to change your lifestyle as you become richer and richer, evolving to a closer and more stable relationship with God which will allow you to do things you never dreamed would be possible. Your wealth will increase abundantly, allowing you to share your opulence with others. In addition, there is a no-lose clause; you're guaranteed to go from rags to riches, from hell on earth to a heavenly paradise. Knock and the door shall be opened, ask and it shall be given, seek and you shall find God's waiting hands.

Man today is suffering from a tragic and inhumane experience, caused by his religious, educational, political and social systems under the spirit of err. It has led to continuous frustration and unimaginable suffering. The tempo and pace of destruction is a sign in itself that we are in the hour of judgment.

The process of redemption for the days of the Kingdom of God does not begin with the Messiah trying to save all humanity, although this is the ultimate objective. He begins his mission in the midst of his people to start the human earthly experience with life by living his words. Thus, the Messianic Plan for the beginning of the new world has begun in the Holy Land, just as sure as the sun rises and sets. The time has come, the Word of God has become the major destabilizer, and judgment has begun at the House of God with the Children of Israel. "He that overcometh and keepeth my works unto the end, to him will I give power over the nations: and he shall rule them with a rod of iron." (Revelation 2:26-27)

I again remind you that a spiritually significant remnant of the Children of Israel, or the Messianic people, can be found among African Americans. Having said that, let us now review some startling events during the contemporary freedom struggle of African Americans. In most instances, they totally reject the idea that their historical past includes being descendants of the House of Israel. In contrast, Herbert Armstrong, publisher of the magazine Plain Truth, states that Great Britain and white America are the lost sheep of the House of Israel. Naturally, Blacks accept his claim as true. A subtle hostility is aroused in African America towards anyone proclaiming that Black America descends from the House of Israel and the substance of the message is lost. Unbeknownst to them, their denial strengthens the hand of their oppressors and prolongs their captivity. They are vegetating in obscurity: no past of pride and no future of hope. Isaiah 1:1-9 compared the intellect of the Children of Israel to that of an ox and a jackass. And it appears that the comprehension of those beasts surpasses theirs. At least the beasts are cognizant of the location of their home. African Americans are not. People all over the earth today are locked in a life and death struggle for land and many struggle in lands that are not theirs. Africa is the world's second largest continent and by far the richest. And the great paradox is that everyone is vying for a piece of Africa except African Americans. It is evident that they are confused regarding their priorities. Their desires are ambiguous to say the least. On the other hand they reject Africa - their land. However, regardless of the extent of my people's ignorance, my Godly-appointed charge is to restore unto the prophetic remnant of them their God-given inheritance as Sons of Light and to open their eyes, ears and minds. But only a fragment will hear and less than that will return unto God. The prophets spoke of a feeble remnant returning unto Him.

The Prophet Hosea, being moved by God, spoke precisely: "My people are destroyed for lack of knowledge; because thou has rejected knowledge, I will also reject thee." (Hosea 4:6) He is definitely not referring to the rudiments of education. If not, then whom or what are they suffering a lack of knowledge of? Is it a lack of the spiritual sensitivity necessary to evaluate the statement of March 4, 1968 by J. Edgar Hoover, outlining the purpose of COINTELPRO? A portion of that memo reads thusly: "Prevent the rise of a Messiah (Christ) who could unite and electrify the militant Black Nationalist movement. Censored might have been such a Messiah; he is the martyr of the movement today." The F.B.I. also wrote: "A man who supports non-violence ought to be destroyed because someday he might abandon non-violence and emerge as a Black Messiah."

In addition to these pronouncements, we should be consciously aware that ten years later, the U.S. policy towards its Black subjects remained consistent. The March 17, 1978 National Security Council Memorandum (N.S.C. 46) under "Policy Options" recommended: "To preserve the present climate which inhibits the emergence from within the Black leadership of a personality capable of exerting nationwide appeal." Did such a policy dictate the final chapter in the life of Marcus Garvey? Did this procedure guide the assassinations of Malcolm X and Martin Luther King? Was the fear of the late Honorable Elijah Muhammad created in the Black community by America's political operatives? Is this same policy alive and well in 1990 concerning Minister Farrakahn? I say, "Yes, most definitely" to the aforementioned questions but I must add that the plot is much deeper and the fear much greater than revealed in those documents.

Why is there an intensive effort to obstruct any systematic movement of African Americans back to Africa? Is this also connected to their attempt to prevent the rise of the Messiah (Christ)? Where were American policymakers' fears and thoughts of a Black Christ (Messiah) born? Something far more complex is coming to play in America's political outlook concerning African Americans. Doesn't it seem somewhat facetious for someone to be watching events and prognoses in the African American communities and connecting them with the coming Savior? Do these things sound absurd? They shouldn't because American and European prognosticators have forewarned the political leadership of the inevitable rise of the Messiah (Christ) from amongst the lost sheep of the House of Israel being held captive in the United States of America.

*"The coming of Black people from America to the Promised Land will be the vanguard of the Messianic Age."*

**Oscar Goldberg (1885-1952)**
**German Jewish religious scholar**

There is no lack of knowledge concerning this coming attraction amongst Europeans and Euro-Americans. Why is there a great void in Africa's theological history? It is as if their first contact with God was upon their arrival in the Americas, while in actuality, it seems that it was in America that all contact was lost.

The essence of man's Messianic expectations must have, as an integral part of that hope, the knowledge that two opposing forces are monitoring prophesy and events while attempting to determine the Messianic season, the Messianic individual and the Messianic nation. Their reasons are as far apart as heaven and earth. There are those waiting to rejoice and join hands; the others are waiting to make war. Please do not be naive. Remember, a Messiah for Blacks in America portends evil for Euro-America as noted in their policy statements. Everyone asking about the Messiah isn't his friend. That now brings me to my final point which has to do with the anti-Christ (enemy of Christ-Messiah), to be distinguished from the "many antichrists" [I John 2:18,] (individual non-believers mentioned in the inspired writings in both the Old and New Testaments). We hear much talk of this figure in evangelistic circles, although the dissertations are very nebulous concerning this enemy of the Messiah. The anti- (enemy of) Christ definitely has to be someone that has much to lose by His coming to establish a new world order. The anti- (enemy of) Messiah will not be some despot with a personal vendetta against the Savior. The anti-Messiah is a <u>system</u> - not an individual - a system that has established itself as lord and master over this planet earth. Iraq, Panama, Iran, Nigeria, Libya and Colombia, no doubt, have some misguided or evil elements, but those countries are just pawns. They have nothing at all to do with the moving of the pieces. They have nothing to do with the policy of the Euro-gentile world government. Any attempt to send you off seeking the anti-Messiah in those countries is to vainly keep you pre-occupied and confused.

Truthfully, if an anti-Messiah came to power in Iraq, what could he do? Who would he influence? Let us take an example from something very familiar to most people in the U.S.: the often-seen pictures and posters of an individual called "Uncle Sam". When I was a child, I thought the very common-looking image with goatee, clad in red, white, and blue, pointing to passersby and calling out "Uncle Sam wants you" was a member of government...someone very important and influential. It was much later in life that I discovered that "Uncle Sam" was the government, the entire system imaged in the personage of a man called "Uncle Sam." I am using this example to emphasize the point I am making concerning the anti- (enemy of) Messiah (Christ). That personage isn't an individual at all; it is an evil, established government system that will oppose any other system attempting to supplant it. Let us be truthful and realistic, as is author Kirkpatrick Sale in his searing biography of Christopher Columbus, <u>The Conquest of Paradise</u>. He frankly relates Columbus' "discovery" of the New World as "the journey that began the long process by which a single culture came to dominate as never before all the other cultures in the world to impose its language in their mouths, its clothes on their backs, its values in their hearts and to accumulate to itself the power that now enables it to determine nothing less than the destiny of the world."

If there is an anti-Messiah (Christ), it will/could only be of the Euro-American/Euro-gentile world. After all, no one else has a world today to defend or that could feel threatened. Understanding that, the final confirmation of our prognosis is that the anti- (enemy of) Christ (Messiah) is the Euro-American/Euro-gentile world government. This world system, with its imposing and powerful armies, fleets and technologically-insane weapons of destruction, is often externally religious, scientific and elegant but internally seething with opposition to God, Truth and right. Commercial warfare is common throughout their economic systems. John the Revelator also makes mention of this awesome power under the influence of the spirit of err.

*"And I stood upon the sand of the sea, and saw a beast rise up out of the sea, having seven heads and ten horns, and upon his horns ten crowns, and upon his heads the name of blasphemy.*

*And the beast which I saw was like a leopard, and his feet were like the feet of a bear, and his mouth like the mouth of a lion; and the dragon gave him his power, and his throne, and great authority.*

*And I saw one of his heads as though it were wounded to death; and his deadly wound was healed, and all the world wondered after the beast.*

*And they worshipped the dragon who gave power unto the beast; and they worshipped the beast, saying, Who is like the beast? Who is able to make war with him?*

*And there was given unto him a mouth speaking great things and blasphemies, and power was given unto him to continue forty and two months.*

*And he opened his mouth in blasphemy against God, to blaspheme his name, and his tabernacle, and them that dwell in heaven.*

*And it was given unto him to make war with the saints, and to overcome them; and power was given him over all kindreds, and tongues, and nations.*

*And all that dwell upon the earth shall worship him, whose names are not written in the book of life of the Lamb slain from the foundation of the world.*

*If any man have an ear, let him hear."*

**Revelation 13:1-9**

## The Rise of the Messiah: The Myth and the Reality

The Euro-gentile network of economics is baffling; all of the earth's wealth and resources are under its control. This network alone dictates your daily value and status; the price of your cocoa, coffee and rubber; your diamonds, gold and silver. They tell you if you are rich or poor, small or great, smart or dumb. You can only purchase with their currency, sell with their permission. They alone make your economy live or die, breathe or suffocate. All of the planet's people are in pursuit of their monetary images. No one else on this planet controls anything of substance.

Every human being striving to succeed has to have the Euro-American/ Euro-gentile mark of excellence or seal of approval. Let no man deceive you. The system or government of sin has revealed itself and opposeth and exalteth itself above all that is connected to God. No one else of their own motivation, other than the Euro-gentiles, has any reason to oppose a new world order, for they have no present world order. The Euro-gentiles represent the only internationally accepted image. That then is the image that has to be challenged. They are the ones who will oppose that change; they are the anti-(enemy of) Messiah (Christ).

In our attempt to unveil this supposedly evasive anti-Christ (enemy of the Messiah) image, let us always keep in mind that there are two Messiahs (Christs) that must come: the Messiah (individual) which was born from the Messiah (Christ) nation and the Messianic nation itself. Being cognizant of that will greatly assist us in our search, for if you cannot identify a/the Messiah (Christ), you'll never find the anti-(enemy of) Messiah (Christ). So the first objective has to be to identify to some extent the Messiah (Christ). Once having some direction in that crucial area, we shall have a clearer picture of who this enemy of the Messiah is.

Let us take a hypothetical example for the sake of strengthening our reasoning. If we had determined that the Messianic nation (House of Israel) was among those people commonly called African Americans, then the enemy of the Messiah (Christ) would have to prevent their being resurrected and reconnected to their God. By doing this, he effectively prevents the spread of salvation through the establishing of the Kingdom of God. That being the case then, J. Edgar Hoover's statement can be placed in a clearer context. We better understand why he states that the American policy is to prevent the rise of the Messiah (Christ). The rise or coming of the Messianic individual (Christ) has to precede the rise of the Messianic nation. A policy to destroy any African American leader that could possibly unify and electrify his people becomes comprehensible (i.e., King, Malcolm, Garvey, Muhammed).

The renowned saying, "There is nothing new under the sun," is definitely a valid expression. Compare the past and present events relating to the Messiah (Christ) and the opposers of his birth. After King Herod heard the prediction of the three wise men from the East according to the information discerned from the stars that, "a Hebrew king had been born," he summoned them to his abode at Jerusalem and inquired of them diligently concerning the matter. Afterwards Herod demanded that they bring him word of the child's location, that he may come to worship him. His plan failed, however, and he was extremely distraught. Consequently, he issued a decree demanding that all Hebrew children two years and under that lived in and around Bethlehem be killed, in a futile effort to cut off the Messiah (Christ). Unquestionably, Herod's primary objective was to foil the probability that the Hebrew king (Messiah) would inspire the masses of Israelites behind him and ignite a new doctrine in opposition to his.

Therefore, who is the anti- (enemy of) the Messiah (Christ)? The anti- (enemy of) Messiah (Christ) is not a figure that just appears upon the coming of the Messiah. He has disguised himself as an Angel of Light and his ministers as preachers of Righteousness as they attempt to prevent salvation from reaching those crying to be saved.

In closing, allow me to reconstruct the Messianic journey. The Messianic personage is born of the Messianic nation. "Unto us a child is born." He then is anointed by God to preach good tidings to the meek; to open the prisons and free the Messianic nation. They must then bear witness to the coming of a Savior and let their light shine before men that they may glorify His Holy name. The center for all of this activity will be Jerusalem - the coming habitation of justice for all men.

*"And I beheld another beast coming up out of the earth; and he had two horns like a lamb, and he spoke like a dragon.*

## The Rise of the Messiah:  The Myth and the Reality

*And he exerciseth all the power of the first beast before him, and causeth the earth and them who dwell on it to worship the first beast, whose deadly wound was healed.*

*And he doeth great wonders, so that he maketh fire come down from heaven on the earth in the sight of men,*

*And deceiveth them that dwell on the earth by the means of those miracles which he had power to do in the sight of the beast, saying to them that dwell on the earth, that they should make an image to the beast, that had the wound by a sword, and did live.*

*And he hath power to give life unto the image of the beast, that the image of the beast should both speak, and cause that as many as would not worship the image of the beast should be killed.*

*And he causeth all, both small and great, rich and poor, free and enslaved, to receive a mark in their right hand, or in their foreheads,*

*And that no man might buy or sell, except he that had the mark, or the name of the beast, or the number of his name.*

*Here is wisdom.  Let him that hath understanding count the number of the beast; for it is the number of a man: and his number is six hundred three-score and six."*

**Revelation 13:11-18**

The above-mentioned verses, in fact this entire chapter in the Book of Revelation, is relating allegorically to a diversified serpentine beast. This beast represents in actuality the world's political systems that are the arena for contemporary satanic activity that plague man and society. For the sake of clarity concerning this man-beast, we must go back to his origin in the book of Genesis, where the serpentine man-beast is first conceptualized. (Chapters 2 - 4).  The vast majority of people equate the serpent written about in these chapters in Genesis as a mere snake - a talking snake, at that.  But it is crucial to realize that the serpent referred to is not a writhing reptile.  Again, I emphasize, this beast symbolizes the world's political systems.

50

The Vision of John recorded in the book of Revelation, is a stark reminder of the continued existence of the man-beast character spoken of in the garden at the time of the creation. The serpent was the embodiment of a rebellious species or segment of the creation. Of this family, the serpentine clan was the most shrewd, sly and cunning. (Compare the seven-headed, one of which is wounded, ten-horned serpentine beast and the very harmless appearing, two-horned, lamb-like serpentine beast.) They were/are contemptible persons who showed/show willful disobedience to and disrespect of God. This very ungodly demeanor caused them to be allegorically referred to by God as beasts of the field.

The "serpent" that approached Eve in the garden to question the instructions given unto Adam by God concerning the trees of the garden engaged Eve in a colloquy, in the course of which she became ensnared and forgot her instructions, becoming spiritually blind at that very critical moment. Thereafter, according to the more accurate Hebrew version, satan deceived Eve and caused her to become a vessel of deception within the society of the Sons of Light. As the cycle goes she then proceeded to deceive Adam and this cycle of deception has continued to this day as we read the book of Revelation.

This incident in the Garden of Eden provoked God and caused His wrath to fall upon the serpentine seed (the rebellious segment of the family of men) and the Holy seed. The "serpent" was cursed downward and given his habitation with the fallen, the treacherous; to be looked upon with greater displeasure and disfavor than all the other loathsome creatures.

Adam and Eve were condemned to suffer the "Process of Deterioration" from which they could only be saved by a redeemer sent by God. God also told the serpent that he would put enmity between the two seeds, thus separating the serpentine seed and the Holy seed, and setting the tone for the struggle between good and evil, the Sons of Light and the sons of darkness. As the plan of God continued to unfold, Adam is used to impregnate Eve, and thus to bring forth in the flesh the substance of the two seeds that she had allowed to be impregnated in her mind in the Garden of Eden. Thus were born Cain and Abel, representing the serpentine seed and the Holy seed.

We see from the events that followed (Cain killing Abel) that Cain was the continuity of the serpentine seed. God thus informed Cain that his dominion would be the reign of sin. In sharp contrast to that, we read of Eve being impregnated once again, giving birth to Seth whom Adam said was the rebirth of Abel. To Seth was born Enoch. Enoch called upon God; he represented the lineage of the Sons of God. The Messianic Light would heretofore shine through the reincarnated seed of Abel (Seth). The serpentine seed was then driven from the midst of the African Edenic family, marked and made to appear as one without father and mother. This satanic spirit became vindictive, setting out to challenge God and to make His chosen a disgrace before His eyes.

In the Garden of Eden, the Holy One of Israel used a limited number of characters by name to act out His message that, in its entirety, would unfold in the generations to come.

We now note that the characteristics of the allegorical serpent-man-beast have been consistent from Genesis to this very day. He is averse to God and Righteousness; he is the father of a lie; sly and cunning. With Eve, his character revealed a collision of ideas; with Abel it was revolt and conflict; with Job we witness polemic and disputation; in the heaven of John (Revelations 12:7-8) we see open rebellion and insurrection. The serpent-man-beast also likes to argue and polemicize.

Have you ever considered how one so openly rebellious against God could be capable of hiding? How could it be that there's a deep mystery concerning his identity? The opposite seems true and much more logical to me. There is no way you could not see something or someone so overtly anti-God except that you are spiritually blind or being led by the serpent in your search. If the serpent is leading you, then he has deceived you to search for something or someone that doesn't exist. That is to say simply, that the serpent-man-beast has no tail, horns, hooves or the literal number 666 inscribed in his head as depicted in the movie "The Omen." We shall now resort to the Holy tongue, Hebrew, to consider this number. We are instructed by John: "Here is wisdom. He that has understanding shall consider the number of the beast, for it is the number or personality of a man and his number or character is six hundred, sixty and six" or 666. Therefore we are advised that someone of understanding could properly calculate those numbers and identity the allegorical serpent-man-beast.

To count the number 666 in Hebrew, we must use the Hebrew alphabet:

| | | | |
|---|---|---|---|
| The First letter | (ת) pronounced Tah-v | = | 400 |
| The Second letter | (ר) pronounced Raysh | = | 200 |
| The Third letter | (ס) pronounced Sahmek | = | 60 |
| The Final letter | (ו) pronounced Vahv | = | 6 |

When we reach the number 666, it forms an intransitive verb: תסרו . Using the root of this verb, ת - ר - ס , we derive the definition from Hebrew to Hebrew and Hebrew to English:

$$תרם = התקוממות, התפלס$$

To oppose, contradict, conflict, clash; a collision of ideas, an uprising, revolt, insurrection, rebellion, polemic, arguing, argumentation, disputation.

We can form a transitive verb by putting it in the active causative form. In the present tense it becomes the person. Example: מתרים pronounced matreese, which means an opposer, contradictor, rebel, one that conflicts in opinion, disputes, etc. II Thessalonians 2:3-4.

Let he that has understanding not search for this number externally, but internally; not on his forehead, but in his mind. For the flesh profits nothing, it is the spirit that quickeneth. By his fruit you shall know him.

The instructions to make an image unto the beast again causes us to focus in on the ultimate objective of satan, which is to supplant the God of Creation. His methods have been consistent down through the ages: to master lying and deception, and to become so proficient in his profession until detection would be rendered almost impossible. Deception has been so effective and extensive until even at this very critical epoch in history there is no longer a conscious perception of an active enemy force which is working to destroy this planet earth. This commonwealth is continuously planning, acting and creating hostility towards God. This is not a fable or myth as most people may think.

# The Rise of the Messiah: The Myth and the Reality

In the book of Revelation, when John notes the creating of a new image, he was not speaking of merely a latter-day plan. His message was to give us insight into an ongoing struggle between God and satan, good and evil, the Sons of Light and sons of darkness. We find our first Biblical account of an image being created in Genesis 1:26-27: "And God said, let us make man in our image, after our likeness; and let them have dominion over the fish of the sea, and over the fowl of the air, and over the cattle, and over all the earth, and over every creeping thing that creepeth upon the earth. So God created man in his own image, in the image of God created He him; male and female created He them." God then described His servant to be perfect and upright, one that feareth God and escheweth evil. Satan, the opponent of God, then countered and formulated his objective - to cause the Sons of Light, those chosen as upright servants, to curse God to His face or disgrace the God who fathered them. Through his evil plan, satan has ferociously attacked the God-image and created a world of his own for his own. "For thou hast said in thine heart, I will ascend into heaven; I will exalt my throne above the stars of God. I will sit also upon the mount of the congregation, in the sides of the north. I will ascend above the heights of the clouds; I will be like the Most High." (Isaiah 14:12-14)

Thus, satan disguised himself and his ministers, after which they devised ways to influence the earth's inhabitants, teaching them to create a new image and forsake the God-image. He commanded that all men should be made in the image of the beast (allegorically, a commonwealth of ungodly nations). This new image was made to challenge the Genesis image, the image of God and Godliness that was perfect, upright and preferred good over evil. This new image of liberal, undisciplined ungodliness would curse God and be a disgrace unto Him. When John made us aware of the conspiracy, the plan had been in effect for thousands of years but was not to reach its zenith until the dominion of the Euro-Americans and Euro-gentiles. It was during this reign that evil made its international debut to a standing ovation of deceived nations. Suddenly wrong - sin - was no longer an outcast but a normal part of a newly defined lifestyle.

The power and authority has/had been given to the image of the beast. The evil image with its crown and glory began to speak and rationalize ungodly behavior, ostracizing all that were opposed. The new image has brought affluence without spirituality to the transformed family of nations. This new standard has brought out the worst in people, causing them to despise the God presence while being possessed with greed. All the world marvels at the power of the forces of evil; the inhabitants feel they owe this new image thanks and appreciation for all of their modern accoutrements. There is at this time a most powerful, organized world of unbelieving men ready to oppose the call for a return unto the God image. The cavalier, ungodly men do not appear openly destructive to opposing ideas. They are always willing to offer compromise or just complicity with evil - a very innocent appearing, subtle defeat for the unsuspecting soul. In this world of darkness it is common to see the supposed believer and unbeliever united in a common purpose.

Evil has spread the length and breadth of this world until all the world's inhabitants view any call for separation as an illusion. "Who can separate from the image and survive?" they ask. This present predicament helps us to focus much more clearly on the events occurring during the end of this world. The end of the world does not imply the total devastation of the earth. It suggests the end of the civilization that controls the minds of men and influences nations; the end of the image or acceptable standard of evil and a return to Genesis and the original plan of creation for a world governed by men governed by God - the end of evil imperialism. You may compare my feelings with those of Moses after receiving the tablets containing the keys to life and being told of Israel's blasphemous act of building the golden calf and declaring it to be their god. He thought, "forgive them, for they know not what they do." But upon his return and seeing them happily rejoicing and merrily dancing for an evil image, he became irate, shaken and traumatized. He was agape; they were actually enjoying the fruit of their iniquity. It is the same when I am given different reasons by African American, African and other community leaders as to why we should remain in the Euro-American/Euro-gentile image which holds us in opposition to God.

I could initially have accepted this as a correctable error in understanding, but when I see them happily participating in the creativity of falsehood, enveloping themselves in thoughts of partnership with and sharing of evil to the fullest extent with the same man whose forefathers raped, stole and enslaved their ancestors, this is not acceptable. The evil that once not so long ago had to be forced upon the African American slaves now finds open acceptance as they have become active enemies of God. The truth is that you are enjoying your new, liberal, undisciplined, ungodly image. Your soul is in an evil captivity and instead of being disturbed, you are happy. After carrying out the will of the rebellious people ("make us gods that shall go before us") by constructing the golden calf, Aaron built an alter and proclaimed, "tomorrow is the feast of the Lord." (Exodus 32:5) But was it truly a feast of the Lord or had this image caused them to identify with Apostate religion?

Apostate religion has been implanted into the minds of the people as part and parcel of the plan of the decisive whole to deceive them and confuse the meaning of the Genesis command "to make in the image of God". The multiplicity of contemporary Christian denominations and associate religions were contrived to cast a quarrelsome shroud over the true image of God by causing disputing ideologies to war against each other. The controversial question is: who is it that has the keys to the true image of God and how will we know with so many variations and claimants? In this question we find the need for the Messiah and the reason the vast majority of staunchly religious persons will reject him. Yeshua (Jesus) said, "by their fruits ye shall know them." Every tree has to bear according to the seed that was planted. "Even so every good tree bringeth forth good fruit; but a corrupt tree bringeth forth evil fruit. A good tree (seed) cannot bring forth evil fruit, neither can a corrupt tree (seed) bring forth good fruit." (St. Matthew 7:17-18)

The way to discern seems so obvious, so simple, so plain until even the fool cannot err. How many people really desire to know and accept the Truth, considering the changes that will be required to turn back unto the image of God? So much has been lost; so little has been gained. The doubt of Eve has caused incalculable suffering. A modicum of faith in these words will yield unimaginable blessings. Why did we forsake that produced by the seed sown in us by the Almighty God? Who is it that has sown the seed that has yielded so much evil? Behold your trees bear gall. Who has ploughed up our paradise and

56

planted the seeds which have brought forth this hell on earth? The image of God, the Father of your existence was to be your everlasting companion. You can have no interest in that of which He is not consulted (considered); no life which He cannot share. If God cannot share your life He shall not maintain it. Strengthen your hands in the works of the Creator of the heavens and the earth. Choose the destiny that was chosen for you by God. When you do, your aims and aspirations will change to those of a people preferring to live under the rule and authority of God. A new beginning, a new Genesis..a new image.

*"And for this cause God shall send them strong delusion, that they should believe a lie: that they all might be damned who believed not the truth, but had pleasure in unrighteousness."*

**II Thessalonians 2:11-12**

# PROGRESS

*To move forward; to develop a higher, better, or more advanced stage.*

# The "CIDE" Series

**CIDE**

The act of killing, destroying, eliminating, eradicating, etc. by means of inflicting adverse elements, environmentally, biologically, psychologically, physically, economically and/or politically.

**PSYCHOCIDE**

The destruction of the mind; miseducation, mental retardation and derangement.

Psychocide is one of the elements that has been activated in contemporary times resulting from a continuous consumption of poison, chemicals from food stuffs, drinking water, preservatives, etc. All these factors have resulted in the deterioration of the brain cells and tissues.

**GENOCIDE**

The act of eliminating a particular race of people or ethnic group, etc. by means of inflicting adverse conditions upon them, i.e. poverty, elimination via nefarious schemes, war, etc.; pitting individuals of different minority groups against one another, committing acts of violence upon one another; encouragement of drug consumption, distribution and addiction; incarceration, political, social, and/or cultural warfare.

**HOMICIDE**

The killing of one human being by another. The murder of one person unjustly or without provocation. Homicide has become commonplace in much of Western society, fueled by intolerance, greed, envy, intrigue, lust, strife and lies. Much of this anxiety and frustration is found in minority areas and communities, i.e. England, United States, and other so-called liberal democracies.

**SUICIDE**

The taking of one's own life. This element of "cide" or death is prevalent mostly in the industrialized nations where materialism has flourished and anxiety has brought on depression, suppression, disappointment, frustration and oppression.

**FRATRICIDE**

The act of killing one's brother, friend, or neighbor. This form of killing has become commonplace in Western societies, particularly increased due to the rise in drug trafficking and consumption.

**ECOCIDE**

The destruction of the Earth by means of the polluting and contaminating of the Earth's Ecosystems, i.e., the rain forests, water system/waterways, atmosphere, etc.

**CHEMICIDE**

To kill or to cause illness by exposure to toxic chemicals. This particular element is associated with nitric dioxide, florocarbons, and other toxic chemicals which are released into the environment and ecosystems from the dumping of industrial waste and the expelling of exhaust fumes from cars, factories, and heavy industry into the atmosphere. These chemicals assimilate into the clouds and return to Earth in the form of acid rain, destroying forests, soil and plant life over the whole world, causing irreparable environmental damage. Mankind is not fully aware of the dangers of this modern day dilemma because of their inability to relate to the extreme dangers of this element.

**INSECTICIDE**  Chemical agents of various compositions found in fertilizers and sprayed-on crops to enhance food production. The chemicals penetrate the soil and are assimilated into the plants, creating biological hazards which harm the consumer and animal livestock.

# Chapter II

# Truth And The New Genesis

*Truth will set you free...when you use it wisely, truth turns men to righteousness, and righteousness turns men to God!*

**Prince Ahkeazehr**

I write words as I am inspired by God - the Holy One of Israel - in order to disseminate His light upon the path that will direct men to find their way back unto God and life. This message of inspiration and the comfort of God's word has to carry you far beyond the immediate emotional refreshment that comes about during the moment you hear or read these words. My words are to prompt long-range action in your life, causing you to make the necessary changes which will in turn bring you closer unto God. I call this the acceptance of Truth. What do I mean by Truth? Truth, correctly interpreted, encompasses the instructions of God as set forth in the Bible. However, Truth generally goes "against the grain" of the lies and deceptions that have become a way of most people's every day lifestyle. For example, most people believe the worship of God occurs one day in the week. That is a lie. The Truth is the worship of God is an ongoing 24-hour-a-day activity that cannot be separated from anything you do.

When one begins to comprehend the dynamics of Biblical, prophetic Truth, it is the beginning of a totally new experience, unlike anything one has ever known because comprehending and adhering to God's instructions entail changing your life. Why? It goes without saying that if we had all been following God's laws, commandments and instructions, there would be no need for books like this or interpreters like me. Furthermore, there would be no war, crime, pollution, waste, broken marriages, homosexuality, families in disarray, extinction of plants and animals, or any other of the numerous unmentionables that besiege us. It is more than evident that man has not been adhering to God's instructions. The problem, therefore, is that the vast majority of people are totally rejecting God's Truth or trying to fit this "new found" truth into their old, devilish way of life.

It is hard to change, even when there is an open admission that the former manner of living and worshipping was wrong. When many find the right answers they won't apply them to their way of life because they conclude that the sacrifice (of not living/doing as society dictates) is too great to undertake. Subsequently, they naturally prefer to hang on to as much of the old, yet familiar and comfortable ways of life, as possible (i.e. worshipping God only on Sundays). They have fond memories, established traditions and so many experiences of joy from the past or old way of doing things until it is absurd - offensive - to suggest changing even though the old way means a life of perversion, killing and wanton death, abundance for some and deprivation for others, the proliferation of diseases, war and destruction, backbiting, lying and disrespect among friends and family; truthfully, the list is endless. The primary reason for the rejection of change is because humanity fears Truth. If the worship of God means rejecting the worship of position, power and materialism, they want no part of Him. These three priorities now dictate man's every action and thought. The worship of God is subtly defined as an impediment to joy, happiness and fun. Yet, want it or not, Truth has now come crashing through inherited religious ideas and pre-conceived notions of right and wrong. It has challenged comfortable beliefs and called into question your entire way of life. Truthfully, with the acceptance of Truth, you are going to miss some aspects of your old way of life for years to come. It will be a true test of your faith. Will you turn away from this required new way of thinking, feeling and doing - even though it is right? It will often seem like an unwelcome intruder...and if this new way of looking at your life - your government, your leaders, the way you eat, discipline your children and relate to your spouse - does not take root in you, you will find yourself resenting it.

The Truth will appear to be your enemy; the lie your friend. That causes people to prefer (in many instances, though they recognize the logic and practicality of the Truth) to cling to the acknowledged lie.

*"Be astonished, O ye heavens, at this, and be horribly afraid, be ye very desolate, saith the Lord.*

63

*For my people have committed two evils; they have forsaken me the fountain of living waters, and hewed them out cisterns, broken cisterns, that can hold no water."*

**Jeremiah 2:12-13**

*"And he spake also a parable unto them; No man putteth a piece of a new garment upon an old; if otherwise, then both the new maketh a rent, and the piece that was taken out of the new agreeth not with the old.*

*And no man putteth new wine into old bottles; else the new wine will burst the bottles, and be spilled, and the bottles shall perish.*

*But new wine must be put into new bottles; and both are preserved.*

*No man also having drunk old wine straightway desireth new; for he saith, The old is better."*

**St. Luke 5:36-39**

In essence, you cannot have both worlds nor both ways. You can't meet God halfway; He demands total commitment. Now, in addition to learning this new Truth, comes the responsibility of making some painful decisions. Don't compromise. Remember, things never get better alienated from God. Whatever way the Master Deceiver (the devil) makes it appear, things are only getting worse. God, the Father of His creations, is not going to change your life for the worse. Eyes have not seen, neither have ears heard what God has in store for those that return unto Him.

## INCORRECT TRANSLATION

*"But the heavens and the earth, which are now, by the same word are kept in store, reserved unto fire against the day of judgment and perdition of ungodly men."*

*"But the day of the Lord will come as a thief in the night; in which the heavens shall pass away with a great noise, and the elements shall melt with fervent heat, the earth also and the works that are therein shall be burned up.*

64

*Seeing then that all these things shall be dissolved, what manner of persons ought ye to be in all holy conversation and Godliness, Looking for and hasting unto the coming of the day of God, wherein the heavens being on fire shall be dissolved, and the elements shall melt with fervent heat?*

*Nevertheless we, according to his promise, look for new heavens and a new earth, wherein dwelleth righteousness."*

**II Peter 3:7, 10-13**

## CORRECT INTERPRETATION

*Moreover the Heavens and the earth, that are before us are concealed (hidden) with His (God's) word and they are preserved (kept) for the fire of Judgment Day and destruction of ungodly (wicked) men.*

*But the day of the Lord will come as a thief in the night; then the heavens in uproar[1] (confusion, ruins) shall pass away and the elements (fundamentals - rudiments - foundations) shall melt from fervent heat, the earth and the works that are upon it shall be burned up.*

*Now if all of these shall dissolve, it is extremely (exceedingly) necessary for you to walk in Holiness and piety.*

*Waiting for the coming of The Day of the Lord, even hasting it, for because of it the heavens are melting in the fire and the foundations are burning and dissolving.*

*Nevertheless we, according to his promise, look for new heavens and a new earth, wherein dwelleth righteousness.*

**II Peter 3:7, 10-13**

How does a thief in the night prepare? Is there much fanfare when the thief is about to carry out his tasks? As a matter of fact, the thief

---

[1] Uproar: A word with root meaning of: (1) to crash into ruins; (2) to be in uproar, to rage; (3) to be ruined, laid waste

plans to catch you unaware. The deeper the sleep, the easier the task. He comes at a time unexpected. He enters in a manner whereby he can move in and out, pick up the valuables and escape. Unless you have been warned and accepted the warning that there are thieves in the neighborhood, you won't be prepared to protect your goods (wealth, life). The pursuit of money, a big car, clothes, lavish home and fun has so diverted your attention until you can no longer halt long enough to turn your attention to the destruction which has subtly crept into every locale, family and individual around you. All of this happened while you were out at the party.

The Day of the Lord coming as a thief in the night implies that either the inhabitants were stone drunk and didn't wake up, or they were not home - possibly out having fun. Or, perhaps they were all caught up in the Super Bowl or a World Cup game. When a thief enters, his objective is not to carry away your home - just all of your valuable possessions.

How does this little scenario relate to Truth and God? It is my objective to open your eyes to the damage the spirit of wickedness - satan - has done to you on a personal level. The devil didn't stop at Adolf Hitler or Ivan Boesky when searching for a vehicle through which he could wreak havoc. The spirit of unrighteousness and perversion has stolen your children's innocence and caused your 14 year old daughter to come home pregnant or your spouse to have an affair. While you were partying or watching the Super Bowl, satan brought drugs into your neighborhood and turned your son into the neighborhood dealer.

Satan - the Master Deceiver and arch adversary of God - is not the mythical character depicted in horror movies and fairy tales that frightened you as a child. Satan is a negative spirit, an adversarial force working against the Omnipotent and righteous spirit and the force of God Almighty. The devil is the force of evil, wickedness, war, death, crime, hatred of God and fellowman - the epitome of all things negative and destructive. These vile characteristics and situations manifest themselves in the actions and thoughts of men. Therefore, when "old Harry" sets out to promulgate his wickedness, it isn't the red-clad, devil with horns and pitchfork that goes about his mischief; more than likely it is your neighborhood car dealer trying to wheel and deal you out of your hard-earned money; your child's nemesis, the bully next door; your state politician making promises he cannot and will not keep; your adulterous spouse; or in many instances, you who has been chosen as the vehicle to do satan's evil.

How do we know that this is the Day of the Lord, the day when God opens your eyes to the great damage satan has done? Check your homes for your valuables. Your closeness with God: gone! Your man and his manliness: disappeared! Your health which was once your wealth: the wealthier our society, the sicker and more disease-ridden it becomes. They even got away with that. Now you're sitting in your big, ten-room home with all of your valuables gone, searching for your insurance policy and your bank book, while at the same time trying to cover the embarrassment by assuring your friends that it's merely a temporary setback and that you'll get over it in a short span of time. Yet, while you're trying to save face, the neighborhood is in shambles; it looks like everyone has been hit.

"Enough is enough", you say. "What is there left of my life?" Then in walked your very distant neighbor, looking joyful and well-nourished. He thus apprised you, "They didn't take anything from my house. It was just a stroke of luck; you can get all of that back and more. Don't worry, be happy." Deception is evil masquerading as good. Things won't get better. In fact, they never have, away from God.

This is the Day of the Lord. This is the same Day of the Lord spoken of by Yeshua (Jesus) of Nazareth. He saw in his vision of the End of the Age the same dullness of ears, blindness of eyes and a prevalent atmosphere of apathy toward Truth and God's way of life. This atmosphere has been superimposed upon the earth's citizens through miseducation or education without the law (instruction) of God. Simple Truth has become imperceptible, while a lie is fashionable and acceptable. A great testimony to the power of miseducation can be found in North America's African American. Their former history, which leads to Northeast Africa's ancient Hebrews, has been obliterated. They have a historical record unlike any others. There's no way to confuse their history with that of other people. Yet, they can read their own Biblical history and not recognize it. They are totally oblivious to a past before the captivity in the Americas. Just as the Euro-gentile has attempted to disconnect ancient Egypt (Mizraim) from Africa, Mizraim (Egypt)

67

from Ham, Cush from Ethiopia, Black and handsome Solomon from his father, David and Yeshua (Jesus) from Israel and Hebrewisms, he has successfully severed African America from their ancestory and historical rememberance.

Few Black Americans (African Americans) are aware of their historical ties to ancient Israel, Northeast Africa (see Foreword, <u>God, the Black Man and Truth</u>) because it was the intention of the Euro-gentile (as a manifestation of the anger of God Almighty at our forefathers' disobedience to His laws and instructions) to destroy the remembrance and historical connection between African Americans and Solomon, David, Ham, Cush and Yeshua (Jesus). There are, thank God, a smattering of Blacks, however, who are aware of the historical ties between the ancient Hebrews, Black America and Africa. The proof of the connection can be found in the Hebrewisms of West African traditions emanating from the West Africans whose ancestors were sold into slavery in the Americas. The ancient Hebrews (Israel) were God's chosen people - the true sons and daughters of God. Nevertheless, Hebrewisms will not be the only characteristic used to refer to those who are the Sons of Light (Servants of the Creator God, men and women with the God-mind) in the last days or the Messianic Age. It has never been the objective of the prophets to term everyone a "Hebrew Israelite". Revelations of God have come to many men of other nations, as evidenced by the similarities of Truths written by many other authors not of the Nation of Israel. The key, however, is to understand that there has been a universal fall in which all men fell out of the favor with God or turned aside from the old ways of our/their fathers into a state of corruption, angering God Almighty. Satan took advantage of this break between Israel and God. Satan, however, did not satisfy himself with just the fall of Israel; he has deceived the whole world.

Satan's plan of deception, in conjunction with the fall of man (from the time of Adam), has mushroomed over the centuries until we have now arrived at these end days. The end of these days does not mean the end of all life on the planet but as it was in the days of Noah when God brought about the Great Flood, and also during the time of Abraham and his nephew Lot who escaped the destruction of Sodom and Gomorrah, the end days will mean an end of an evil age of a government of men governed by satan, according to God's plan.

Therefore, as God has always had a Universal Plan (Noah and the Flood, for instance), so has God's message also been a Universal Message. The Master Teachers (sages of God's word, the prophets of old, Sons of Light) are aware that at the end of the Euro-gentile age there would be a need of a <u>new</u> Genesis (beginning). This new Genesis will not be a re-creation of flesh as in the first Genesis. It will be a re-establishing of the Order of God. The Prophet Isaiah spoke of darkness over nations and over contemporary scholars - a void in Godly intellect or the understanding of God's instructions as written in the Holy Scriptures. He spoke of an age in total chaos under the rule of satanic-minded leaders, educators and formers of social patterns (inventors, designers, advertisers, etc.)

Everything has to be re-ordered under the mind of God. The earth is off its axis, reeling to and fro under disorder. Man today is completely void of the understanding of the Order and cycle of God. Man does not know what to do with gold, silver, the Amazon, the rain forests, the fertile lands, the food that is grown, the wildlife, etc. Man does not know how to use contemporary modes of transportation (and avoid pollution), or telecommunications without disrupting the wildlife, exposing man to radiation or destroying the forests. Man has sacrificed the earth's wealth (natural resources, minerals, etc.) for the sake of man's wealth. In this world of the continuous pursuit of money, power and materialism the earth's inhabitants do not know how to relate to each other. The woman of God is gone, the man of God is gone and their children are lost. True love is dead!

When the conditions are clearly understood, the need for the New Genesis will become comprehensive. Man has to be re-created in the image and likeness of God. His societies will have to be re-ordered to compliment God, nature and people - not materialistic wealth. There has come a new beginning; a world governed by men governed by God; and a society set in order by men set in order by God; and a home established by the God-family wherein children honor their father and mother, woman respects her man, and man is in the image of his God.

The warning to repent from the life-destroying, perverted patterns that have become the norm today is coming from many different countries and sectors of society (the environmental protection agencies, the societies for the prevention of cruelty to animals, to name a few). God, being a God of Order, has merely set the order for the universal struggle against the forces of evil. We find that order being referred to in the book of Isaiah, the 2nd chapter. We (Israel) were chosen not just to provide light or guidance of God for our numerically small selves, but to provide the same light or guidance unto all the nations. Satan's influence has crept into all countries and religions. As a matter of fact, he has used religion to turn men away from righteousness. The fact is that religion has been very subtly substituted for right (righteousness, Truth, the Laws of God). It is the job of Hebrews, or the Children of Israel, to shine a light of correct social, political and spiritual behavior on the lifestyles of all men, to inspire the master teachers to become active again, while realizing that in all societies there will have to be an overhaul of all of the mechanisms in use to worship God. It will not necessarily be the physical seed of Israel who revives the spirits of other nations, but the center of that revival will most definitely be Jerusalem.

A salient point of reference is that all master teachers know that veganism once was the proper diet of humanity and that there will have to be a return to sound dietary principles. Yet, in all societies there has been a great deception concerning dietary habits. In other words, where once man survived healthfully and nutritionally on fruits and vegetables, nuts, grains and seeds, now if one doesn't have a fat, juicy steak on his plate, the meal is not complete. Yet, that steak is actually a portion of a dead animal that has begun to decay (everything dead begins the process of decay from the onset of death). Any nutrients that may have been in the living animal begin to dissipate the longer the cut of meat sits. The nutrients are further lessened by the cooking process. And the dietary deception doesn't begin and end with meat. Carcinogens (cancer-causing properties) are alive and well in almost every processed, preserved item you purchase from the grocery store. In a nutshell, if you are not eating a fresh vegetable or fruit, you are more often than not killing yourself. We must move from religious dogma to righteous lifestyles with very different and varied cultural expressions.

# Truth and the New Genesis

There will soon come a time when all men and nations will be referred to as Sons and Daughters of God, Sons and Daughters of Light, one universal family under God, the Holy One of Israel. Even though Yeshua (Jesus) of Nazareth was mainly teaching and living in an Israelite environment, His message was universal and an indictment against contemporary religion and religionists.

*"Think not that I am come to destroy the law, or the prophets; I am not come to destroy, but to fulfill.*

*For verily I say unto you, Till heaven and earth pass, one jot or one tittle shall in no wise pass from the law, till all be fulfilled.*

*Whosoever therefore shall break one of these least commandments, and shall teach men so, he shall be called the least in the kingdom of heaven; but whosoever shall do and teach them, the same shall be called great in the kingdom of heaven.*

*For I say unto you, that except your righteousness shall exceed the righteousness of the scribes and Pharisees, ye shall in no case enter into the kingdom of heaven."*

**St. Matthew 5:17-20**

*"For God commanded, saying, Honour thy father and mother; and, He that curseth father or mother, let him die the death.*

*But ye say, Whosoever shall say to his father or his mother, It is a gift, by whatsoever thou mightest be profited by me;*

*And honour not his father or his mother, he shall be free. Thus have ye made the commandment of God of none effect by your tradition.*

*Ye hypocrites, well did Isaiah prophesy of you, saying,*

*This people draweth nigh unto me with their mouth, and honoureth me with their lips, but their heart is far from me.*

*But in vain they do worship me, teaching for doctrines the commandments of men."*

**St. Matthew 15:4-9**

Yeshua (Jesus) said clearly that he did not come to destroy the vision and the dream of those worshipping God in other nations, but he came that the vision might be realized. Yet, he admonished them to take heed, for the righteousness of the righteous would have to exceed (or go far beyond) the religion of the religionists who have adopted traditions which have made the Worship of God of non-effect. Yeshua (Jesus) was neither against the law nor Moses. He had observed a situation wherein the law, as the overseers had allowed it to develop, had lost its effectiveness as the vehicle for maintaining a close relationship between the people and God. So many new traditions had crept in and been superimposed on the law of God that the laymen had, in actuality, lost both God and the law. Yeshua's (Jesus') ministry could thus be seen as a prototype of a struggle between the way of God and the contemporary customs of men.

The greatest burden on a messenger of God is when his people do not understand his mission. Subsequently, they allow his enemy to define him, his mission and purpose. Thus, the people judge him not by what they perceive and recognize him to be, but by the distorted image portrayed by his foes. This process of definition destroys the process of deliverance and perpetuates the conditions which the messenger of God has challenged. Therefore, in most cases where religion is concerned, the true worship of God is not being undertaken, but rather a man-made, "anything goes" version of what the "powers that be" feel the people should be doing, which is not the way it was in the past. For example, the early followers of the carpenter from Nazareth celebrated the Biblical feast days handed down to them through the Children of Israel. They did not celebrate Christmas, Easter nor Sunday as the Sabbath Day. These changes evolved during the centuries of transition from an eastern to a western, God-influenced to satan-influenced, African-influenced to Euro-gentile-influenced church (or we could say from the ways of Yeshua (Jesus) to the will of Constantine). The Euro-gentile even went as far as to create another Jesus as he turned the people away from the historical, Biblical Yeshua (Jesus). He moved him out of a way of life founded upon the laws of God to a new Jesus who was the father of a new Euro-centric Christianity. To be Messiah (Christ)-like initially meant a return unto God and the original intent of the law. Today, after hundreds of years of orchestrated, racially-based deception, the Euro-gentile is now faced with the monumental decision of having to tell his children the truth concerning the original man and all the ancient forefathers (Noah, Abraham, David, Solomon, Yeshua (Jesus)) being black men, or cut them off from access into the New World.

It is easier to change a wrong habit to right than to change a wrong religious habit to right. Furthermore, it is easier for a camel to go through the eye of a needle than for a staunchly religious individual to enter into the Kingdom of God.

The term "Easter" was not used nor was it known by early Christians. And, the word translated as "Easter" in the Acts 12:4 (King James Version) is in fact the Hebrew word "passover" or "Pesach". The present pagan holiday can be traced to the ancient Babylonian worship of Astarte, the Queen of Heaven, and Ishta, worshipped by the Assyrians. The early followers of Yeshua (Jesus) saw themselves as adherents to his faith in the God of Israel. They had no need to change the customs as set forth (and later written in the Old Testament) by the ancient prophets who received instructions from the Holy One of Israel Himself. Yeshua (Jesus) held them within the sphere of influence of the revelation through Israel. After all, these feasts' (Passover, Feast of Weeks, Feast of Tabernacles) authenticity had been ratified by Yeshua (Jesus) in the New Testament. Thus, it is evident that he meant or would have them to do the same. Paul himself was an Israelite, and in believing, he never stopped believing the Old Testament as being the Word of God.

After all, the Epistles of Paul did not exist but were compiled centuries later. They were never written as a part of a/the Bible. They were merely words of inspiration to his followers for those times. You read his letters and then tell me which Holy Days he advocates celebrating. You will find no new feast days being celebrated or advocated other than those passed down through the Ancient Israelites.

*"But this I confess unto thee, that after the way which they call heresy, so worship I the God of my fathers, believing all things which are written in the law and in the prophets:*

73

*And have hope toward God, which they themselves also allow, that there shall be a resurrection of the dead, both of the just and unjust.*

*And herein do I exercise myself, to have always a conscience void of offence toward God, and toward men.*

*Now after many years I came to bring alms to my nation and offerings.*

*Whereupon certain Jews from Asia found me purified in the temple, neither with multitude, nor the tumult.*

*Who ought to have been here before thee, and object, if they had ought against me.*

*Or else let these same here say, if they have found any evil doing in me, while I stood before the council.*

*Except it be for this one voice, that I cried standing among them, Touching the resurrection of the dead I am called in question by you this day.*

*And when Felix heard these things, having more perfect knowledge of that way, he deferred them, and said, When Lysias the chief captain shall come down, I will know the uttermost of your matter.*

*And he commanded a centurion to keep Paul, and to let him have liberty, and that he should forbid none of his acquaintances to minister or come unto him."*

*"And now I stand and am judged for the hope of the promise made of God unto our fathers:*

*Unto which promise our twelve tribes, instantly serving God day and night, hope to come. For which hope's sake, King Agrippa, I am accused of the Jews."*

*"Purge out therefore the old leaven, that ye may be a new lump, as ye are unleavened. For even Christ our passover is sacrificed for us.*

*Therefore, let us keep the feast, not with old leaven, neither with the leaven of malice and wickedness; but with the unleavened bread of sincerity and truth."*

**Acts 24:14-23, 26:6-7 & I Corinthians 5:7-8**

It was only in later centuries that forces hostile to the domination of African thought and leadership in ancient theology severed the ancient Israelite influence and moved the center of the newly emerging Eurocentric religion to European capitals. New World religious theology originates in European capitals. A quote from Constantine indicates the spirit of the Roman Church at its beginning. "We ought not therefore to have anything in common with the Jews for the Savior has shown us another way...In unanimously adopting this mode (Easter Sunday) we desire, dearest brothers, to separate ourselves from the detestable company of the Jews." (Life of Constantine 3:18-19) There was opposition to his break by some who understood the unceasing need to adhere to the roots of the rich olive tree.

*"And if some of the branches be broken off, and thou, being a wild olive tree, wert grafted in among them, and with them partakest of the root and fatness of the olive tree;"*

**Romans 11:17**

*"That at that time ye were without Christ, being aliens from the commonwealth of Israel, and strangers from the covenants of promise, having no hope, and without God in the world;"*

**Ephesians 2:12**

But the seat of authority was to be moved in accordance with the prophecy of Daniel 7:25-26. Thus it did happen; the wild olive branch became dominant and from its fruit came this Evil, religious world.

# Chapter III

# From The Garden Of Eden To The Garden Of Evil

Only when the African American unequivocally desires to be redeemed will the chains of slavery begin to fall away. Only then will he follow a champion of God who will guide him in the process of redemption and reconciliation with the Holy One of Israel. Does the African American (or humanity, for that matter) really believe in Biblical, prophetic redemption? The answer is most definitely No! Could there be anticipation without preparation? If you believed in the necessity to make a journey to another city, for example, would you not be preparing for your journey? How much more preparation would be made if you were anticipating a journey to another world? Wouldn't it be intelligent to familiarize yourself with the way of life there? How could someone be preparing to live with God without great interest in His way of life? True anticipation motivates preparation.

Why does it sound so strange to your ears the words, "If you love God, act like it! If you love justice, act like it! If you love one another, act like it! If you want to be redeemed or delivered, simply act like it!?" How would you feel about someone saying they love you while acting like they hate you or saying they want freedom while acting like they love being slaves? Is your moral and ethical development to impress God or satan?

In the same vein, if there is to be a deliverance, the people must be accountable unto someone sent by God who is easily recognized as God's chosen messenger. He would have to have Messiah (Christ)-like attributes, not worldly qualities. This Messiah will be the obedient servant to the Plan of God. He will be accountable unto God. Know of a surety, however, that it is the objective of the forces of the evil sons of darkness to make the people reject the Deliverer, preventing them from being obedient to God's instructions. The Bible teaches us of

76

many Messiahs or Deliverers coming at certain epochs in the history of Israel. Noah was the anointed of God in the days of and preceding the Flood. We read that as Noah taught of destruction and deliverance, there was apathy towards him and his message. The people proceeded on with business as usual.

With every rejection of a deliverer, those to whom the message came experienced further suffering and catastrophe. When the Almighty entered into a covenant with His people who were to be a light unto all of the nations, he made it known that He would be found by them if they sought Him. If they forsook Him, He would forsake them. Furthermore, in the course of their relationship, the people would always receive much more than they gave. This would be the goodness and mercy of God. This message, though, has always been the same from Noah to Yeshua (Jesus) of Nazareth: You must put forth some effort in order to receive the deliverance of God.

Yeshua (Jesus) said your house is left unto you desolate, in ruins, until you put forth an honest effort toward its rehabilitation. This process of decay would continue beyond the day of Yeshua (Jesus), on to the end of the Euro-gentile dominion. Then there would occur a significant historical change. The message of the final call would be: to reject the Deliverer would cause a cataclysmic destruction to fall upon all humanity. Yeshua (Jesus) said, "no flesh would be left alive," but thanks be unto God in the days of the Kingdom of God that a sufficient remnant of the House of Israel and other Sons of Light will accept their savior in the midst of much clamor and opposition, thus shortening the time. For the sake of these elect of God, time will be shortened, stopping just short of total destruction for all humanity. This elect will bear witness of his coming and herald the doctrine of the Kingdom, starting what I call the Cycle of the Latter Days of Euro-gentile Dominion.

As I continue my explanation begun in the previous chapter of the very important message of Peter concerning the end of this age, I must remind you that the Euro-gentiles have twisted the cross and the scriptures into weapons of disenfranchisement. It is for this reason that Euro-centric theology and religion have not brought us even a semblance of salvation, nor strengthened our relationship with God. The Hebrew scriptures or Biblical verses written in Hebrew carry with them a living spirit whenever they are significant or true (not distorted). They come alive and meet whoever is of Truth and confuse those who are not of Truth.

When these words come alive and inspire the messengers of God, they are taken on a journey into the souls of those who spoke them or wrote them. Yeshua (Jesus) said, "those of Truth can hear Truth, and a strange interpretation they shall not follow." David also said, "Behold I come in the volume of the book, for it is written of (in) me, I delight to do Thy will. O my God: yea Thy law (Truth) is within my heart." The Truth of what was meant is written in the hearts of the messengers of God. When the Holy One of Israel elevates a savior, He anoints him with the keys to open the door that allows him to enter His realm (Hosea 12:10).

In most instances, the Euro-gentile, because of self-deception, cannot enter this sacred realm; therefore, his exegeses and hermeneutics are only based on the corporeal. Thinking that they have become wise, they have instead made themselves fools. Instead of moving upward, their motion is downward. In their present carnal state of existence, the lower the moral requirements and level of God-consciousness, the more they like it. They have a very low standard of living, self-esteem and self-respect in the eyes of God, the Creator of the Heavens and the Earth.

*"But thou, O Daniel, shut up the words, and seal the book, even to the time of the end: many shall run to and fro, and knowledge shall be increased."*

*"And he said, Go thy way, Daniel: for the words are closed up and sealed till the time of the end.*

*Many shall be purified, and made white, and tried; but the wicked shall do wickedly: and none of the wicked shall understand; but the wise shall understand."*

**Daniel 12:4, 9-10**

*"To the law and to the testimony: if they speak not according to this word, it is because there is no light in them."*

**Isaiah 8:20**

78

*"For the people shall dwell in Zion at Jerusalem. Thou shalt weep no more: he will be very gracious unto thee at the voice of thy cry; when he shall hear it, he will answer thee.*

*And though the Lord give you the bread of adversity, and the water of affliction, yet shall not thy teachers be removed into a corner any more, but thine eyes shall see thy teachers:*

*And thine ears shall hear a word behind thee, saying, This is the way, walk ye in it, when ye turn to the right hand, and when ye turn to the left.*

*Ye shall defile also the covering of thy graven images of silver, and the ornament of thy molten images of gold: thou shalt cast them away as a menstruous cloth; thou shalt say unto it, Get thee hence."*

**Isaiah 30:19-22**


The lowering of the level of God-consciousness was part and parcel of the Euro-gentiles' wickedness, by all means, but it is important to understand that this was merely part of God's Divine and Holy plan. In anticipation of the times of the gentiles, He sealed the Holy word until the time of the end. How were the writings of the law and the testimony of the prophets Divinely sealed until the time of the end? We can be certain that the sealing of this book was not a corporeal undertaking with corporeal materials, yet here Daniel has expressed the will of God to close the canon. How was this accomplished?

The Euro-gentile was allowed to develop his new religion basically unchallenged during the times of the Gentiles' reign over God's people and creations. During the development of his religion, as with everything else during his rise, racism came into focus. He, realizing that the canon of the Old Testament showed greatness and favor to Africa and Africans almost in its entirety, thus formulated a theology of darkness concerning African people. As one of its cornerstones, he declared the Old Testament to be fulfilled, making it unnecessary for study by laypersons. Any layperson caught diligently studying the ancient canon would most definitely be ostracized. Here again, those with eyes to see can discern the infinite wisdom of God. The book was placed on the family bookshelves and sealed until a set time in the great plan of God Almighty. Therefore, we realize that the sealed book referred to by Daniel the prophet is the Hebrew canon of God. In the last days of Euro-gentile rule, the prophets would again begin to speak. They will come alive again in the doctrine of the Kingdom of God. You will once again hear the echo of the words of Yeshua (Jesus): "I have not come to destroy (continue to deny) the law and the prophets, but to fulfill." The messengers of God will place the law into its proper context, heralding the good news of the establishment of the long-awaited Kingdom of God. Humanity shall hear the Truth and the Truth shall set them free from the death grip of satan.

Hear, O Israel, and all humanity. It does not matter if you are underclass, middle class, or upper class. You are the victim of an overdose of miseducation. I am earnestly trying to flush it out of you. The process is complex but except that I succeed, the process of recovery cannot/will not begin. The process of recovery will be long and arduous; many of your vital organs have been infected. Recovery is still possible but you will have to swallow this bitter flushing agent I am giving you. And what is the alternative? Well, except that you hear, you will never live to know that there was one.

> *"Son of man, I have made thee a watchman unto the house of Israel: therefore hear the word at my mouth, and give them warning from me.*
>
> *When I say unto the wicked, Thou shalt surely die; and thou givest him not warning, nor speakest to warn the wicked from his wicked way, to save his life; the same wicked man shall die in his iniquity; but his blood will I require at thine hand.*
>
> *Yet if thou warn the wicked, and he turns not from his wickedness, nor from his wicked way, he shall die in his iniquity; but thou hast delivered thy soul."*
>
> **Ezekiel 3:17-19**

After close perusal of the aforementioned verses of the epistle of Peter, we find a frightening correlation between the more accurate translation and the prevalent conditions of the world and its inhabitants. It should leave no doubt that we are actually in the time period called "The Day of the Lord". This being the case then, the sons of darkness (those who perpetuate satanic rather than Godly principles) are in the last or final phase of their downward motion. It is also very significant to take note that the magnitude of the evil that has been wrought upon the world was hidden from discernment, allowing the time of the Gentiles to run its course in accordance with the Word of God. Now in this, the Day of the Lord, the revelations of the unending, unbelievable evil that has been perpetrated upon the planet are coming to the light and believe me, they are mind-baffling. It seems that man's continuous thought is to do evil. Evil is a disease of the mind. The sick, degenerate mind has created sick, degenerate societies. Isn't it ironic that a whole world of people are taking the same road to destruction at the same time, in the same way, with the same religions as their mentors, the same education as their teachers and leaders, with each blaming the other for the world's condition and future destruction?

*"Professing themselves to be wise, they became fools,"*

*"Wherefore God also gave them up to uncleanness through the lusts of their own hearts, to dishonor their own bodies between themselves:*

*Who changed the truth of God into a lie, and worshipped and served the creature more than the Creator, who is blessed for ever. Amen.*

*For this cause God gave them up unto vile affections: for even their women did change the natural use into that which is against nature:*

*And likewise also the men, leaving the natural use of the woman, burned in their lust one toward another; men with men working that which is unseemly, and receiving in themselves that recompense of their error which was meet [AIDS].*

*And even as they did not like to retain God in their knowledge, God gave them over to a reprobate mind, to do those things which are not convenient;"*

*"Who, knowing the judgment of God, that they which commit such things are worthy of death, not only do the same, but have pleasure in them that do them."*

**Romans 1:22, 24-28, 32**

What is being referred to through the use of the metaphors "Heaven and Earth" (II Peter 3:7, 10-13), when we thus read, "The heavens and the earth that is before us has been concealed (hidden)."? It means that the realization of their intent was not obvious. The inhabitants of this planet earth were completely oblivious to what was being perpetrated. We need not be exceptionally intelligent to conclude that you cannot hide the literal heavens and earth. Wherefore we are thus certain that it has some symbolic meaning or significance. What are and where are the heavens and earth spoken of metaphorically in the prophecies and epistle of Peter? Heavens = the high place, origin and source of intelligence, the mind of man. Earth = the lower place, land, habitat of your works and deeds; the place to show the substance of your thoughts and origin of your mind.

Now as we review the writing, it becomes much clearer: the Heavens (minds) in uproar, in confusion and that are raging shall pass away. In addition, the earth and the evil works that originated in the evil mind shall be burned up. The mind behind this world, or that produced this world and the works born out of it, must die.

I am sure many still do not comprehend what I mean by the sick, degenerate mind. I could not possibly be referring to the upstanding *Good Housekeeping, Ebony* magazine citizens who attend church regularly, donate faithfully to the March of Dimes or volunteer as den mother or father for their community scout troop.

Well, to further enlighten your sick mind, consider the following achievements your sick society has produced:

- The **Mind** that is destroying the tropical forests, home to at least half of the earth's plant and animal species at the rate equal to one football field a second.

- The **Mind** that legally exports to less informed countries, a product (such as cigarettes) that has been confirmed to be dangerous to the health, as if their citizens are not considered humans.

- The **Mind** that legalizes prostitution and homosexuality.

- The **Mind** that dumps tons of food items into the ocean to protect price stability, while others starve.

- The **Churlish Mind** that teaches men and women... "Modern Western society still preserves some old myths about menstruation, all of which can be ignored. It is perfectly safe for the menstruating woman to bathe, shower, swim, wash her hair and have intercourse, and take part in any other activity she wishes."[1]

- The **Mind** that is purposely wiping out life on earth.

There is no technology available to prevent the killing, maiming, robbing, dope peddling and exploitation of one another. Scientists will not find a cure for broken hearts, heart ailments and heart attacks. Neither will they be able to cure cancer or find a "safe" pill for birth control. Consider the mindlessness of men and the darkness of governments that employ thousands and spend hundreds of millions trying to find a safe, healthy way to alter or prevent God's will from being fulfilled. Trying to circumvent God is a plan destined for failure. I state clearly, emphatically and authoritatively that there is no injection discovered or yet to be discovered which will allow mankind to continue smoking, polluting and consuming poisons while not being afflicted with cancer. There is no safety in wickedness.

Yet, so-called Third World or "underdeveloped" countries are continually being seduced to embrace the "progress" of the West. Shamed into rejecting the natural as primitive, backward or lazy, they allow

---

[1] WOMAN'S BODY, AN OWNERS MANUAL - Paddington Press Ltd., 1977 N.Y.

themselves to become "developed" away from the righteous cycles of life.

The one person that should certainly take heed when good health is mentioned is the woman because within the human family, no vessel has undergone so much abuse as that of the woman's body. It is a wonder that she has any body left at all, after the chemical aerosol sprays and deodorants used externally and the cancerous tampons and douche concentrations used internally. She has had her tubes tied, her ovaries removed, foams sprayed internally, pills swallowed, hysterectomies, mastectomies, caesareans and abortions.

She has waged war against God and lost. All of the abominations mentioned could have been prevented simply by believing and following God's instructions; but instead she rebelled against Adam and followed the law (instruction) of the devil and made herself an enemy of God. It is no wonder then that today all women are suffering from what is called "female sickness." Disease exists in the female sex organ at a ratio unparalleled in history. Venereal disease has become so pandemic until certain viruses are now being passed on to the young daughters, who have become victims of their mother's disobedience unto God; subsequently, those in their early and preteens are now experiencing "female troubles." Some of these viruses are virtually incurable and when detected, the women are advised to discontinue childbearing.

Yet, the fact remains that AIDS (and other venereal diseases) are the end result of the carefree lifestyles, promiscuous attitudes and permissive environment promoted during the "sexual revolution" of the 1960's and '70's. Sexually liberated, we are now "free" to contract any number of evil afflictions. The subsequent rise in female troubles, gonorrhea, syphilis, herpes, chlamydia and AIDS has made the sexual revolution a modern-day "Trojan Horse."

How can we see diseases of this sort and not consider them a plague upon the people? In former times, something so widespread would have immediately caused people to begin repentance and seek God for an understanding of what they had done wrong. Today, there is no true fear of God because God is only seen in the abstract and not the absolute. Religion has left you void and in darkness concerning God

Truth and Worship. Everything suffers: your mind, spirit, and physical body.

> *"Notwithstanding I have a few things against thee, because thou sufferest that woman Jezebel, which calleth herself a prophetess, to teach and to seduce my servants to commit fornication, and to eat things sacrificed unto idols.*
>
> *And I gave her space to repent of her fornication; and she repented not.*
>
> *Behold, I will cast her into a bed, and them that commit adultery with her into great tribulation, except they repent of their deeds.*
>
> *And I will kill her children with death; and all the churches shall know that I am he which searcheth the reins and hearts: and I will give unto every one of you according to your works."*
>
> **Revelation 2:20-23**

> *"Behold, I am against thee, O thou destroying mountain, saith the Lord, which destroyest all the earth: and I will stretch out mine hand upon thee, and roll thee down from the rocks, and will make thee a burnt mountain.*
>
> *And they shall not take of thee a stone for a corner, nor a stone for foundations; but thou shalt be desolate for ever, saith the Lord."*
>
> **Jeremiah 51:25-26**

As humanity heads into the last decade of the 20th century, man finds himself at a crucial turning point. The actions of those of you that are reading these words at this very moment will determine the future. Man, under the influence of the era of Euro-gentile dominion with his mind trained in science and computer-age technology, is applying his education to the perfection of weapons of death. His capacity for destruction has become almost unlimited as evidenced in the recent Gulf war. Why hasn't the European used his awesome influence and vast wealth to enhance Truth and the influence of God? Why doesn't he demand a right way of life as a prerequisite for gaining his support and assistance? Why doesn't righteousness command a high level of respect in his societies? Why is corruption and destruction so rampant? Does he subtly encourage injustice and unrighteousness? If so, why?

Francis Fukuyama insinuated that the final world government would be something akin to a "secular paradise" - not spiritual, not Godly, and not righteous but earthly and materialistic, omitting God. God had sent him a strong delusion, causing him to believe a lie. Who would have as his objective or dream that an ungodly paradise would be the final form of human government except the man of sin, the son of perdition? If not God's Kingdom or Paradise, then whose kingdom is this to be? "Even him, whose coming is after the working of satan with all power, signs and lying wonders." (II Thessalonians 2:9)

Who opposeth and exalteth himself and his world beyond the promised paradise of God? Paradise was once the Garden of Eden where God placed those created in His image. Now we hear talk of another paradise wherein satan, the opponent of God, will place those made in his image. It is evident that we have now come to the end of our journey on this planet earth, from the Garden of Eden in the beginning to the garden of evil in the end. Euro-American, Euro-gentile liberal democracy, with the promise of a fast-moving, all-inclusive techno-synthetic world signals the end of humanism, the end of feeling.

The computer takes your payment, gives you your change and thanks you for your patronage. Essentials to modern man's lifestyle are: instant orange juice; microwave popcorn; artificial insemination and hearts; cloning and biological engineering; chickens that can't see, cluck or fly and eat their own waste; a chemical hog and cow; laser printing and operations; fiberoptics; and, of course, crack - a derivative of cocaine produced for Black consumption.

Artificial intelligence and synthetic solutions are seen as progress and no nation can keep afloat except that they are in the image of the Euro-gentile world. The Euro-American, Euro-gentile has set the standards for human behavior for small and great, rich and poor, free and bound. At this particular epoch in history, their world is sought after on a much larger scale than the world promised by the Creator God.

86

*"And no marvel; for Satan himself is transformed into an angel of light.*

*Therefore it is no great thing if his ministers also be transformed as the ministers of righteousness; whose end shall be according to their works."*

**II Corinthians 11:14-15**

*"I, the Lord, have called thee in righteousness, and will hold thine hand, and will keep thee, and give thee for covenant of the people, for a light of the Gentiles;*

*To open the blind eyes, to bring out the prisoners from the prison and those that sit in darkness out of the prison house."*

**Isaiah 42:6-7**

*"And he said, It is a light thing that thou shouldest be my servant to raise up the tribes of Jacob, and to restore the preserved of Israel: I will also give thee for a light to the Gentiles, that thou mayest be my salvation unto the end of the earth."*

**Isaiah 49:6**

*"Arise, shine: for thy light is come, and the glory of the Lord is risen upon thee.*

*For, behold, the darkness shall cover the earth, and gross darkness the people: but the Lord shall arise upon thee, and his glory shall be seen upon thee.*

*And the Gentiles shall come to thy light, and kings to the brightness of thy rising."*

**Isaiah 60:1-3**

The aforementioned Corinthianic epistle is at the zenith of its fulfillment at this present time. Again, we find the opponent of God having thoroughly searched the ancient prophetic writing before preparing his strategy. Therein, he discovered that God had designated a special mission for the House of Israel; they were to be a light (source of Divine intelligence) unto all the earth's inhabitants. He subsequently took advantage of the fallen state of the Sons of Light and in their absence he disguised himself as an Angel (messenger) of Light and his representatives as heralders of good tidings.

Satan, having disguised himself as a source of inspired intelligence, is now able to move in the midst of the human family, deceiving and destroying without detection all of man's life-supporting infrastructure. Satan is a master of deception, making the Truth appear as the lie: I say you're dying, and that your bodies and minds are sickly and disease-ridden; satan says you're living.

All communities talking of discipline, love of fellow man and nature with authoritative leadership are labeled "cults". Those that allow for perversion, the marrying of gays, advocate the consumption of anything and try to stay out of people's lives are called "religious". I point out that there has been a total collapse of morality and ethics in contemporary society, leading even those who appear honest and sincere into sin. You clap for Madonna and declare that you are free. How has deception become so widespread? Simply by institutionalizing wrong, it becomes hard to identify and even harder to condemn.

The opponent of God, after disguising himself as a source of intelligence, realized that intelligence is decimated through institutions. He then moved to take control of the institutions of learning and transformed them into the training arenas for his thoughts. He trained the unsuspecting students to worship (work for, toil for, labor for the fulfillment of) him. After being well-trained, they are trustworthy enemies of God and sent forth full of zeal and energy, ready and willing to destroy the creations and humanity, in search of their pot of gold by destroying the rainbow. His objective was to integrate evil into the system and lives of men until it neutralized any attempt at mass destruction or rejection, for to uproot evil would be to uproot themselves. The earth appears to be so full of light but my warning to you is that it is artificial, synthetic light.

The prophet Isaiah, looking through the eyes of God declared, "Behold, darkness covers the earth and gross darkness the people." Looking out over the Euro-American, Euro-gentile world, what did Isaiah see? He saw man's mind being trained to be his enemy. Remember, your mind can be your friend or your mind can be your enemy. It all depends on how you use it...or better yet, how you're trained to use it.

Do not misconstrue my words as a protest against learning, reading, writing and arithmetic. Learning survival skills is not the problem. In your naive pursuit of survival skills, you allowed yourselves to become ensnared in courses of misapplication of education. Carter G. Woodson called it "The Miseducation of the Negro". I call it the deceptive education of humanity. To deceive is to cause someone to accept as true or valid what is false or invalid - to lead astray. Woman has been led astray from her man, children have been beguiled away from their parents, man has been misled away from God and government has been led away from the laws of God.

The planet has been literally made into hell on earth and no one seems to care. Deceptive education has neutralized all opposition. Truth can at times be very piercing and discomfiting but I must cry aloud and spare not: "And this gospel of the Kingdom shall be preached in all the world for a witness unto all nations; and then shall the end come." (St. Matthew 24:14) This Truth will either convert you or bear witness against you, set you free or reveal your preference to be spiritually blinded. "For if we sin willfully after that we have received the knowledge of the truth, there remaineth no more sacrifice for sins, but a certain fearful looking for of judgment and fiery indignation..." (Hebrews 10:26-27)

We of African decent in the Euro-American captivity have borne witness to the limitations of good education wherein Divine spiritual enlightenment is absent. In America, we have seen the pomp and the poverty of society controlled by the spirit of err. Yet, our salvation is sure but it will be in the manner prescribed by God: "Hath he said, and shall he not do it? Or hath he spoken, and shall he not make it good?" (Numbers 23:19)

There was a time when the crisis of destruction appeared far off, in the far away future of our children. Now it isn't the lifetime of your children; it is occurring in your lifetime. The brunt of the results of the evil, industrialized societies are falling upon you at this very moment. Except that you heed my warning, repent and turn back unto God, you possibly won't survive another decade. At this point, there already is no future for the children. The next knock on the door will be to pick you up. You only have now - not generations - to effect the necessary change. Every living being has to be made aware and given a clear, lucid understanding of the churlish mind behind this nightmare. The laymen have to become active in this struggle; the politicians have sold their souls to the spirit of err. They are, in most cases, the problem personified. The wasteful, careless ways must become a thing of the past. You must reorder your lives and lifestyles.

With the coming of Godly men, a new course is being charted to establish the New World Order. When we say "New World Order," we mean simply a new arrangement of lifestyle and purpose, being cycled back unto God and a life wherein Godly principles will rule supreme. You must restructure your mind in order that you may reorder your day, your purpose in God's kingdom and feelings toward your fellowman.

The order in which things are done may be playing havoc with your emotions, family, pleasures and health; for the order adhered to today was established by men of evil purpose who had no intentions of working in harmony with the Creator or created. They have disdained His cycles, rules and guidelines and have not only cast them aside, but have attempted to destroy them altogether. These men were established by satan to carry out his devilish plot against the Creator, while attempting to supplant God as the supreme authority over the earth and its inhabitants.

So when we say "New World Order", we call into question the present order in which you do things and value things - from yourself to your friends and even your enemies; from your work hours, play hours, drinking hours, study hours, eating hours and rest hours. Everything in the present order of things must be called into question.

How is it possible for you not to have noticed that the present order is not conducive to the creation of family stability, harmony, mutual trust, love, dedication, good health; nor peace of mind, body, society, neighborhood or home? We must conclude that this world's order is not ideal for perpetuating these principles, virtues or effects.

One must be audacious and holy bold to step out onto the path of a world that is bent on a course of destruction and proclaim oneself a pioneer for its salvation. It takes much nerve to say you are the definers, designers, and prophesied governors of God's Kingdom and even moreso to say you are God-commissioned to have the wisdom and vision to be its instructors, guides and saviors. Men of God are not appointed by men to be saviors, prophets and holy men. Saviors become saviors when they, being God-inspired, realize the need of those crying out to be saved from those who have an unholy command of their soul and future.

Now more that ever, the world needs a government of men governed by God, for the corrective measures required must begin with reconciliation with God, that His spirit may be prevalent in the awesome task of turning man back to God and life. The choice is simply to change or face extinction.

# Chapter IV

# The Spirit Of Good And Right

*"Observe and hear all these words which I command thee, that it may go well with thee, and with thy children after thee for ever, when thou doest that which is good and right in the sight of the Lord thy God."*

*"And thou shalt do that which is right and good in the sight of the Lord: that it may be well with thee, and that thou mayest go in and possess the good land which the Lord swore unto thy fathers"*

**Deuteronomy 12:28; 6:18**

We must always remember to reinforce what is good with what is right. The Holy One of Israel merely gives us examples of His light (intellect) to guide us on the path of judgment and day-to-day decision-making. It would not be practical to attempt to list every activity or interaction of man with his fellowman. In the Holy writings, the delineation of a number of representative laws provides the guiding light for things far beyond the immediate situation or activity. In order to administer the way of God, one has to have the all-encompassing spirit of God to guide him. The Spirit of God is the invisible force behind the law that is written and unwritten. Many Biblical verses are merely guidelines for situations that may develop in your day-to-day living. They are not seen as binding commandments. They are, in most cases, materials with which we must build structures. For example, many statements concerning judgment are guidelines for the perplexed. One should always be conscious of his limitations in matters of judgment. Everyone can't judge in every case or jurisdiction. Poor judgment can lead to you being poorly judged.

We must always think and be motivated by the Spirit of Good and Right in the eyes of God. The law guides us by particularizing and generalizing. Thus, one should not cloak himself with the letter of the law while strangling the Spirit of the law. The law is as the universe of man. There is an outer law or layer (the letter) and an inner layer (the spirit). Man has been created in like manner, having the outer body (flesh) and the inner (soul). The things you do outwardly must be motivated by or inspired by the proper reason. For to be obedient outwardly for the wrong inner reason is to violate the law.

Each generation has to interpret and apply the law in accordance with its conditions and exigencies. Yet, it has to always maintain the one original spirit of intent that was and forever shall be. Those interpreting and applying the law must first and foremost be servants and worshippers of the Holy One of Israel, the Creator God. After fulfilling that requirement, we shall be able to discern events taking place around us and will not have to always wait to hear a voice from Heaven beyond the clouds. We shall hear from the New Heaven that has come down into the midst of us; our own God-given and God-inspired intellectual understanding will come into play.

*"Surely the Lord God will do nothing, but he revealeth his secret unto his servants, the prophets."*

**Amos 3:7**


*"The portion of Jacob is not like them: for he is the former of all things: and Israel is the rod of his inheritance: the Lord of hosts is his name.*

*Thou art my battle axe and weapons of war: for with thee will I break in pieces the nations, and with thee will I destroy kingdoms:*

*And with thee will I break in pieces the horse and his rider; and with thee also will I break in pieces the chariot and his rider;*

*With thee also will I break in pieces man and woman; and with thee will I break in pieces old and young; and will I break in pieces the young man and the maid;*

*I will also break in pieces with thee the shepherd and his flock; and with thee will I break in pieces the husbandman and his yoke of oxen; and with thee will I break in pieces captains and rulers."*

**Jeremiah 51: 19-23**

# The Messiah and the End of this World

Let us review a couple of examples of good and right being traversed by good and evil. First, we will consider Europe's contribution to the balance sheet in Africa's social development. The Euro-gentiles contribute a substantial amount of aid to Black African countries, but in a manner planned to create need and dependence. The very same nations then contribute assistance to white South Africa, but in a manner to create independence. The good of aid is only on the surface for both Black Africa and the white South Africans. The white South Africans are then subtly equipped to further the oppressive plan of Europe, while their counterparts - the Black African states - have to submit to oppression. All of this is a result of good gifts motivated by an evil inclination. America's aid programs work under the same shadow of death - good and evil as opposed to good and right. They assist a select element of African Americans to attain higher education and so-called "success", after which they create a high-profile image for them. These individuals are then expected to be bulwarks for social injustice, neutralizing any effective and consistent opposition. This token elite class of affluent African Americans is a necessary public relations control mechanism. The problem is that they did not rise in stature by opposing Euro-America; their gains were on his terms. Now they must think like him, talk like him, reason like him, lie like him and destroy like him. To protect their newly-attained status they must inevitably protect his system of oppression.

When the truth of the evil one's intentions are revealed in books such as these, the Kingdom of God is made to look like a crazed, irrational cult. The oppressor's objective is always to silence all God-inspired opposition to his evil objectives. The reason being that with true opposition would come reason or motivation of opposition. In this case, it involves Truth being revealed and the Lie being uncovered.

When the blind lead the blind, they both merely fall into the pit. Therefore, the blind have to be led by someone that can see. The perpetual hope of the blind man is for eyes. When he that has eyes is shown the correct way to go, the blind have to submit to being led by him. It always returns to the element of relativity. Those seeking God must be led by the Godly, for who you are being led by is relative to where you are going. To concede to be led by the ungodly is to accept your ultimate destination of hell. Therefore, the ungodly are being led by and prefer to be led by the ungodly. The Godly would lead them away from ungodliness. Therefore, the law of relativity demands that if an individual considers himself to be Godly, he must be assured that his leader or leaders are likewise Godly.

*"Can two walk together, except they be agreed?"*

**Amos 3:3**

The ungodly ruler can only succeed if he has at his disposal an ungodly constituency. A blind individual can only lead someone else that can't find his way. The same principle applies to planning and programs. They are the same social traps laid for the people year after year. They are born out of darkness and obscurity. Their social programs are plans for the blind and the ungodly. Their societies are corrupt and the people are trapped. If the people sincerely want help and to be saved, then they must seek someone espousing and undertaking salvation - someone not of their world. Yeshua (Jesus) said, "I have come into this world, but I am not of this world."

In order to prevent true opposition to evil, the evil one gives the impression that a plan of opposition already exists. This and many other subtle methods are used to deceive the struggling Sons of Light and the lost societies. Let us take, for example, an illustration of the American political scenario. First, we have Republicans, Democrats and Independents. Then there are Conservatives and Liberals, Hawks and Doves, Extremists and Moderates. Then in the midst of this conglomeration are the African American, Hispanic and Indian politicians. It therefore contains enough diversity to deceive the carnal eye into believing that somewhere in this array of politicians, there is hope. But just as Marxism and Capitalism are merely flip sides of European cultural tradition, so are the aforementioned all governed by and guided by the same constitution.

The Constitution is the only legal tender; it alone provides the direction and supreme authority. These above-mentioned political parties are not opponents of the Constitution; they merely have opposing views as to how to carry out the same plan. Their tactics differ, but their objectives are one and the same. They are part and parcel of the same political system that was born out of the Constitution. The system itself is the enemy!

"One of the most profound undertakings of the Euro-gentiles is what I term the Great Religious Conspiracy. The Euro-gentiles have deceived the whole world, causing it to honor and worship false gods and idols, while at the same time giving an impression of their superior intelligence and culture; wherein, no one would believe that they are pagans, still honoring the false gods of their fathers. No race of people has so negatively altered the laws, seasons and purpose of God's creation as have the Euro-gentiles, yet they are not seen as criminals that continuously violate the everlasting ordinances of God Almighty. The significance of Judgment Day is surely that the Sons of God will be awakened, to bring this criminal to trial, laying bare all of his evil deeds. We must always remember that satan is wise and a master of evil...a master deceiver.

Europeans rule the world today, and because of this rulership there is no justice, equity, peace, love of fellowman, love of God or true happiness. Instead of everyone accusing him and forcing him to relinquish the Spiritual Magna Charta (authority to rule), everyone continuously attends his conferences and forums, placing their hope in the cause of the calamity. This is a phenomenon if there ever was one!"

**<u>God the Black Man and Truth</u>**

In evaluating European dominion, let us look for one non-European country that is a true friend of Europe. After 400 years of rule, they have not earned the true friendship of even one country or established one country whose works pay homage to the God of Creation. To what do we attribute the friendless European? The truth is that he is cunningly making war with God, His creation and people, as evidenced by the fact that any nation dealing with Europe feels an ulterior, evil motive behind everything she does. The entire non-European race, whether listed as friend or foe, feels a need to defend themselves against her presence: they feel that she is inherently up to something evil!

## The Spirit of Good and Right

The Euro-gentile statesmen and speechmakers are continually promulgating "all men are created equal". This doctrine has the effects of a powerful narcotic. Everyone is quoting the beautiful things the Euro-gentile says, but very few take notice of the ugly things he is doing. If all men are created equal, equality certainly ends immediately after creation because from that day until the non-European meets his grave, everything is inequitable. Every land governed by Euro-gentile persons or principles is sustained by hate and division. Every political system, economic system, social system, building code, industrial code, quality code (poor quality, poor people; rich quality, rich people) and war code breeds inequality. Without the resurrected God-mind, no one understands that all men are neither mentally nor physically created equal.

The educational institutions all over the world today reflect a commitment to Euro-gentile standards and values. They justify and perpetuate the cultural enslavement of all other people. A world that desires to keep us powerless and enslaved cannot afford to give the oppressed the teachings that will free us, nor a God that will save us. A tyrant that desires to keep us weak cannot reveal a history that will make us strong. We initially flocked to their educational institutions seeking the tools needed for our survival and development of our countries and societies; instead we received the tools necessary for the maintaining and further development of Euro-gentile countries and societies and the further strengthening of white superiority.

Without the understanding of Truth, you will have a tendency to feel that the defect is within you personally, that you are the cause of your condition and not the evil government of men under the influence of err. There is an infrastructure clandestinely designed to maintain Blacks and non-Europeans in subordination, whereby the leaders can rely upon it to uphold the injustices of bigotry and racism. Simultaneously, the hypocrites pacify the masses of the Third World countries with false promises. The entire Euro-gentile infrastructure is caste and race-oriented and is not about to be dismantled. The religious system, the educational system, the economic system, the political system and the social system are all active parts of a racist system of government.

Satan has been with us since Genesis. His first action that is written in the Holy Canon was to challenge God. From his inception up to this present time his methods of deception have changed tremendously. He has advisors and lawmakers that render evil very hard to detect. Nevertheless, no one realizes that satan and his evil have penetrated every facet of life to such an extent until even the supposed pious and chaste have been contaminated. Evil is everywhere and has diseased everyone and everything. None of those that have developed mechanisms to help mankind understand that you cannot use the forces of satan to inspire Holiness or Godliness; therefore, you don't help humanity, you help the devil. No matter how it is disguised or how good your intentions, you can only become an instrument to carry out his diabolical plot against the people and the environment - their source of life. Then we have the European scenario: Communism, Socialism, Marxism, Social Democrats, Liberal Democrats, Christian Democrats, Labor and Conservative Parties. Let us briefly consider the opposing Democratic and Communist regimes.

Here now is the paradox. The higher standards of morality and social justice were found in the countries that were supposedly without God. The promiscuity and social irresponsibility is found in the supposedly Christian countries of the West. However, through the eyes of the God-mind, all confrontations that have their origin with God are right against wrong, good against evil, God versus the devil. Keep that in mind as I paint you a picture of reality and profound deception.

Had this struggle between East and West been ordained by God, America's objective would not have been to dismantle Communism, but to merely bring it under the influence of God while demanding that it not only maintain high standards of morality and social justice, but also insist that they share with the West the techniques used to accomplish such a feat. Those in the Eastern Bloc working for a change would have been seeking a better spiritual understanding from the West while wanting to share the methodology of achieving moral sanity. The end result would have left the Eastern social structure mainly intact, yet stronger, while bringing the system under the influence of God. America would have strengthened her social structure while at the same time maintaining - even improving - her status with God. With both blocs, East and West, under God, with stronger morality and more social justice, the victory would have gone to God. Needless to say, this was not the case. It is relatively easy to conclude, therefore, that it was not a struggle between the ultimate forces of good and evil, God and satan, but in-house haggling over ways and means of controlling the planet and its wealth. It was a great victory for the West. The people of the Communist countries still do not believe in God, yet there is more freedom - freedom for greater expression of their dedication to satan and their opposition to God. It can thus be summarized with the statement from the internal opposing forces of hell's house of heat..."Mr. Chairman, we are not in opposition to being evil; we only oppose some of the devilish things we do."

He that has ears to hear, let him hear. This was merely a socioeconomic struggle, not the (nor a) struggle between the Sons of Light and the sons of darkness. This is yet to come.

# Chapter V

# Law, Knowable Truth And Spiritual Energy

*"It is time for thee, Lord, to work: for they have made void thy law."*

**Psalms 119:126**

Why is there a continuous attempt to distort and lessen the significance of the law of God in Euro-gentile religious theology? Why has the law come up for such extraneous criticism from contemporary Christian theologians? The law represents the intellect of God in the realm of man. It gives us a look into the portion of the God-mind that is tuned into the governing of man by the Most High. Therefore, when we understand this, it causes us to be more anxious to seek an understanding of the law than to criticize it.

*"Behold, I have taught you statutes and judgments, even as the Lord my God commanded me, that ye should do so in the land wither ye go to possess it.*

*Keep therefore and do them: for this is your wisdom and your understanding in the sight of the nations, which shall hear all these statutes, and say, Surely this great nation is a wise and understanding people.*

*And what nation is there so great, that hath statutes and judgments so righteous as all this law, which I set before you this day?"*

**Deuteronomy 4:5-6, 8**

David said, "the law is the light." Isaiah said, "Rise and shine, for thy light (intellect of God), has come for darkness covers the earth, and gross darkness the people." This darkness represents ignorance of the

100

law, or being in opposition to the intellect of God. The frightening reality that overshadows the individual's opposition to the intellect of God is that all societies are being governed by constitutions born out of the spirit of err.

Within each society, we find religion and its devastating influence over people's manner of thinking, living and governing. The travesty of religion is that it was designed to mislead. How else could all Christian countries have constitutions not based upon the laws handed down through Moses, the messenger of God, who was made a god unto Pharaoh? These laws are a constitution (or the basis for all constitutions) by which men were to govern upon this earth in their various societies. Nevertheless, the mind that would be used to expand upon the constitution, when need be, would be born out of its contents.

Usually the rejection of the laws of God is based upon an obscure factor such as the animal sacrifices. This is satan's use of deception, because that being the case, only this portion of the law would have been rejected. How did the entire Mosaic Law become subjected to an admonition because of one percent of controversy, while disagreement with points of other constitutions merely leads to the tacking on of an amendment while leaving the basic document intact? Are not the structures of societies today relevant to what is allowed or encouraged by the systems and methods used to govern them? For example, greed is so prevalent today until we must assume that it is somehow encouraged by the basic documents used to govern. Western money-making has become divorced from necessary, constructive industry and the public good. The worship of money is evident throughout the industrialized world. In the words of banker Felix Romatyn: "There's no moral opprobrium attached to the outlandish accumulation of wealth by speculators - even from churches." There is also a quiet consensus that exists among European and Euro-American scholars concerning the Bible. They have asked the questions and then shaped answers within the framework of racial, cultural and general presuppositions they hold in common. This biased consensus has purposely undermined the Almighty God and His Truth, life and salvation. This has confused man's self-understanding and the place in history of other racial and ethnic groups vis-a-vis the House of Israel, the Elect of God.

A portion of that deception has resulted from the ability to dissect the Ten Commandments from the laws (instructions) of God. The master of subtlety has removed, almost in its entirety, the fact that these Ten Commandments are an integral part of the whole Law of Moses. People have somehow forgotten that they, too, came to man historically through the man Moses. They were not born out of, neither do they exist in, a vacuum. Can you separate the seventh commandment of Exodus 20:14 from Leviticus 20:10 or the ninth and tenth commandments of Exodus 20:16 and 17 from their sister commandments of Deuteronomy 19:16-19 and Deuteronomy 22:1-4? The Ten Commandments are part and parcel of one family of law (instruction). Thus, the forces of evil have completely removed the vision of man from the thinking of God in the government of men. This is the primary reason that the earth is in spiritual darkness and the people in gloom. Destruction and corruption are upon the people because of a lack of the basic knowledge of God. As you start the journey back unto God and sanity, you must unequivocally reject the many traditions of the religionists which are not rooted in the law and words of the Prophets.

Many misconceptions concerning the true worship of God have been used to divert men from the path of Truth. They are the desires of men, not the requirements of God. These new traditions often come in direct conflict with the inspired word of God. In many religious communities they even supersede the Torah. This parody did not originate with contemporary religion; it was already highly noticeable during the ministry of Yeshua (Jesus). Many of the newly-added traditions were in fact taking our people farther away from the fundamentals of the Torah. We see a perfect example in the development of contemporary Christianity. Very few individuals are aware that in its inception, Christianity was engendered in the Hebrew (Jewish) community. Its existence began long before the birth of Yeshua (Jesus) (although it was not called Christianity). The main objective initially was to return the masses back to the basic spiritual concepts of the law. It was totally Hebraic in allegiance and vision. Yet, by the fifth century C.E., it had taken on another character and direction. Its Hebraic roots had been severed and its direction had deviated to such an extent that it appeared to be a totally new religion. The original message and objective of the carpenter from Nazareth, Yeshua (Jesus), had been totally misconstrued.

Yeshua (Jesus) himself no longer appeared to be a Hebrew, dedicated to the keeping of the law and obedient to the words of the inspired prophets of God. The same pattern is also evident in contemporary Judaic religious practices.

At this point there has to be a new spiritual rebirth. We must return to the roots. So many things have been grafted to the original tree of life until we just could not be sure of the original fruit it bore. We have arrived back in the genesis in search of the original message and intent of God's law (instructions). The mass deception of the earth's people was preceded by the successful removal of primary sources for life-sustaining information. Once the people were convinced to follow secondary sources, the manipulation of basic life knowledge was made relatively easy. The law was much too personal; it made God too close for comfort; that is, too close for evil to operate comfortably. Evil is only comfortable operating in darkness.

To contemporary man, fashioned in the image and likeness of European concepts and objectivity, it is much better and acceptable if God is distant - if He stays out of their lives just far enough to allow them to do what they want to do. But when He comes near, it disturbs them. They prefer that He remain abstract and amorphous, impersonal, tending to the universe, space or anywhere else far away from them. This is why they produced a new non-Biblical Jesus, according to the specifications of their minds' requirement. He was a "just-have-faith" Jesus, the undemanding Savior that remains on the periphery of your lives and lifestyles; you just call his name. This Jesus came down from another heaven (mind), as hero of another earth. He is used to safeguard the habitation of the wicked instead of to challenge its existence. They allow their Jesus to play a major role every Sunday in exchange for a promise not to interfere with the systematic behavior that they alone control.

> "The white race seeks to create an artificial universe, a universe of "test-tube babies", "artificial brains", "artificial birth", "artificial life", - a universe made and shaped in their own image. This world would exist independently of the control of nature, beyond the control of God. It would be controlled only by their corrosive science and technology. A universe in which they would be God and gods.

In their perfect place, they will determine the order of things from the highest to the lowest levels of existence. A universe in which each creature must be useful to white interest and control. In that space and time whites would seek control over life and death. Most definitely, this universe has no room for any people of color, particularly not Black people."

**White Genocide - Black Obsolescence?**
by Olomenji

What is the primary source of life-sustaining information? It is the Bible from Genesis to Malachi. The secondary source is Matthew to Revelation. As with all things, we must first find Truth, which when accepted , frees us to unequivocally relativize all other things according to that Truth. (See Daniel 9:13; Isaiah 26:2-3; Psalms, 119:142; St. John 8:32, 43-47; St. John 3:19-21; St. John 16:12-13; St. John 18:37). After all of the philosophizing has been done, we must conclude that "Truth" is merely the right knowledge of reality.

The prophets referred to Truth not in the abstract, but as something tangible. David said, "Let thy truth preserve me." The Truth, when known, provides light upon the path and direction for the lost. Yeshua (Jesus) said it would extract freedom from injustice and give comfort. When you rationally consider the state of your family, society, health, environment, and government - in other words, the state of your world - it is not difficult to conclude that neither humanity nor the environment is being preserved. As a result, your children are on drugs, your society is crime-ridden, your health has deteriorated, the ozone is gone and the wildlife is extinct and the government is more concerned about its public relations image than the state of the world. I would venture to say that darkness is prevalent on the path of man. All people have been dominated by an evil, Euro-centric, cultural imperialism and certainly there is no comfort in being ruled by satanic-minded politicians. These things being reality, the Truth has to manifest itself because the people and the environment are under the control of a lie. That being the truth, the implications are that the European mind set, world view and projections are based upon a root formula of lies.

The major problem with humanity at this time is not so much not having access to Truth, but accepting Truth and doing Truth; combining Truth with energy to bring forth its vital substance. Today, the forces of evil have deceived the whole world, wherein men use their energy to bring forth the substance of a lie which causes environmental destruction and self-destruction. Thought is actually matter or energy that, once set in motion, can create or bring forth life and life-sustaining substances, or the reverse-death and death-causing substances. The thought in the mind (word) is actually the object without motion. The heralder of the tidings then has to be skillful enough through Truth or deception to make the listener believe or have faith in his words, to the extent of setting the thought into motion to manifest the tangible. Nevertheless, without the creation of the thought, the energy will not come forth to produce the substance.

In the Biblical Hebrew language, the consonants, dahlet, vayt, and resh (דבר) pronounced (from right to left) "dah"-, "vah"-, and "r" mean "word". The same word also means "thing". From that we may safely deduce that the message of God's Holy language is that words are things without substance. It is the energy of strongly induced thoughts that create the motion that makes them substance. The same three letters in Hebrew also form the root for the verb "to speak, to talk". Thus, we may further deduce that the words (things) that we speak energize the thoughts. This Truth shines a light on our path which leads us to another very significant word: Ah-yen, vayt, dah-let (Ah-vah-d), the Hebrew root of the word which means "to work for, labor for, toil for, to work as a slave, to worship". It can be seen from the definitions that the original message equates work and worship. Thus, the worship of God is defined as one's every good and righteous work, act or deed. Through worship (work) man moves to bring forth substance of thought, for if the thought does not become energy and energy become motion, the substance will not come forth or be made manifest. Where the worship of God is concerned, your every action - cooking, cleaning, welding, composing, brokering, selling (everything that you do) - is an expression of your worship of God. Furthermore, if you are doing something contrary to God's laws (i.e., killing yourself - as it is written, "thou shall not kill" - by smoking cigarettes) you are worshipping satan, not God. Therefore, it is certainly evident that the devil has deceived the whole world into worshipping him. He has been successful in his craftiness by making his world appear tantalizing and by causing man to disassociate his job, business, eating habits, shopping habits and recreational habits from the worship of God. Yet in Truth, all of these actions denote worship. It is only a matter of who is being worshipped...God or the devil. We must certainly reflect back to Genesis and the words (things) spoken by the devil. Through his impressive presentation, he convinced Eve to listen. After listening, a thought became energy and when set in motion, it brought forth substance, which caused the fall and alienation from God. Thus, we draw an analogy from when students or persons come into the presence of messengers of God and listen to them speak the word (things) of God. When they hear, they begin to think and subsequently are energized by the word.

The African and African American has had his ears removed. He only talks in his own world; he does not listen. He is too busy to listen, so consequently his understanding of life and how best to preserve life, prolong and prosper physically and spiritually is constricted and disconcerted. The ox knoweth his owner and the ass his master's crib, but my people won't even consider that salvation can only be set in motion by Truth heard, Truth believed (thought created) and Truth done. Thought coupled with energy will set the word in motion to produce a substance of tangible salvation.

Therefore, when the adversary of God challenges and attempts to destroy the Sons of Light, he is in reality simply trying to stop them from "thinking like that". He attempts to prevent anyone from listening to them by discrediting, killing, maiming or causing fear of the light (God's doctrine) which is also a form of energy. Yeshua (Jesus) said that the Light of God is sufficient in its radiation to give strength to all men that will allow it to shine upon them. The adversary of God is an enemy to all sound doctrine. He has to always have a cause which will create the effects of alienation from God. He creates fear of hearing the words which will cause the thoughts which will produce the energy and motion, thereby yielding the substance of a new world - and thus, bring about his destruction.

> *"Arise, shine; for thy light is come, and the glory of the Lord is risen upon thee.*

*For, behold, the darkness shall cover the earth, and gross darkness the peoples, but the Lord shall arise upon thee, and his glory shall be seen upon thee."*

**Isaiah 60:1-2**

*"The entrance of thy words giveth light; it giveth understanding unto the simple."*

**Psalms 119:130**

*"The people that walked in darkness have seen a great light: They that dwell in the land of the shadow of death, upon them hath the light shined."*

**Isaiah 9:2**

The Holy Oracles were not written to deceive men, but to be a light of understanding on the path to righteousness as the Sons of God seek to come out of their deep coma of ignorance about God, their Father. For many seasons the Sons of Light have been without the True God, the Truth about God, and ears to hear and a mind to absorb the facts concerning God and salvation from their teaching priests. However, only if you are sincerely seeking shall ye find Him. Ask and it shall be given; knock and the door shall be opened. If you are really crying out unto God, you will understand these things which are written and know of a surety that they are true. Surely the God of Truth is displeased with men who have been convinced that they have received revelations (supposedly from Him but which in fact are not from Him). These men must be the products or off-spring of some force that opposes God and His Truth. It is infallibly true, my children, that the knowledge of Truth is and must always be the best friend of humanity. It is the only doctrine that never was and never will be harmful.

Truth never opposes Truth; it agrees or compliments Truth. It only opposes a lie. How does one distinguish the Truth from lies? It's the same gauge used in determining what is right and what is wrong, who represents God and Holiness and who represents evil and wickedness. But for that matter, do you care? In your subconscious mind, do you shrug off a "little white lie" or a little "devilment" as being innocuous? When you read in the paper that Europe banned the importing of U.S. meat products because the meat was hormone-treated, do you side with America in her anger and hostility at Europe over this act because it hurts America, " the land of the free and the home of the brave", or do you separate the truth from the lie, right from wrong?

Truth doesn't just begin and end with the Bible. The absence of or rejection of Truth is seen in all facets of your day-to-day life: in your newspaper, staring back at you through the eyes of your local newscaster, or silently worded on the labels of your food items. Again, if you are really and truly seeking answers to your family crises, social injustice or spiritual indecision, than it is essential that you distinguish the truth from the lies. Are you one of those who believe everything you read in *Time* magazine? Do Ted Koppel, Dan Rather or Morley Safer teach the gospel in your book? Do you accept the current styles, designs, fads and trends because most people have adopted them or do you step back and take a critical look at everything and try to find the God-element in it? If so, then you qualify as a Truth-seeker. And as the end of the century draws near, distinguishing the Truth from the inordinate lies and wickedness will assign you to the proper category in preparation for the last days.

As we now move into the final decade of the 20th century, we are at a very unique historical moment. It is doubtful if there has ever been a time in history when so many institutionalized intellectuals were talking about "the end". There is "the end of history", the "end of nature", the "end of science", and the "end of this world as we know it today". I myself am not discouraged, for the prophets of old spoke of a cataclysmic change occurring at the time of the end of Euro-gentile domination of this planet. We are truly witnessing the end of the artificial world and beginning of the real world governed by men governed by God. The end of this world may mean different things to different people. Some of us have concluded and are thus greatly concerned that the rulers have led humanity to a plateau of evil from which the execution of further evil will be difficult. Total insanity is the inevitable next step and thus, mass destruction of the earth's people could occur.

How will the people know of this imminent catastrophe? I believe that God Almighty in His infinite plan has made Truth knowable. There are comprehensible laws and rules governing the behavior of all matter. We must be able to know God and the devil. There is a relative Truth that governs behavior. Anyone earnestly in search of this Truth, having basic faculties of learning and comprehension, can have this Truth revealed to him. That means any intelligent being anywhere will come upon the same logical conclusions after assembling the Truths concerning this present world system. A primary position from which to begin is the acceptance of the knowledge that all men of God, wherever they may be, are in opposition to this world system. I make this statement, not having conversed with these men; this is my faith in Truth. The forces of evil, darkness and satan do exist. They then must be detectable because the laws governing them forces them to interact in a way that we can observe and discern. This is why the prophets of God continue to warn us of the danger of being blind and deaf. "You have eyes that see not, and ears that hear not." They further stated that the people are being destroyed because of a lack of the basic eye-opening teachings of God as well as an overall complacency concerning God and righteousness, which is as a result of the attention-diverting aspects of our lives, such as television and video. Consequently, the world today is perishing in its sins because God is no longer overlooking our complacency and is bringing our every action into judgment.

Man today cannot grasp, nor does it appear that he desires to grasp, the significance of a positive relationship with God. He cannot envisage another wealth of greater value than all of his combined materialistic accoutrements. Generally speaking, all men are in pursuit of these things, as if materialism and status were actually life itself. Maybe that's part of the problem. Man has been taught that with the accumulation of corporeal wealth, life begins. Nevertheless, no soul can avoid indefinitely recognizing its mistakes. With this recognition comes the fact that you have actually been working and accumulating yourself to death. The material wealth was/is merely the wages for your obeisance unto the devil, the justly culminating effect of which is perpetual damnation and being imprisoned without access to your sense of reason in the society of err.

God the Father has established a universal law. He neither has to chastise or punish, but within the cycles of order and right, you reap what you sow. Man, therefore, makes his mind his friend or his enemy. The world today, we can certainly conclude, is neither a friend nor worshipper of God. Man, not understanding the law of cause and effect, in error blames God for the fruit of his works and labels Him harsh and unjust. Thus, the inhabitants of the planet earth today are in a cycle of self-destruction, as the master deceiver gives them the impression they are really living. But by your own truthful analysis, no one can be in a cycle of life, having turned aside from God. It seems, then, that everyone would just change. You probably would if you were free to accept and understand Truth. But instead you are imprisoned by habits which prevent the intelligent use of your mind. If under the control of satan and his evil system, there are things you consider so precious and worthy of your most outstanding sacrifices, imagine the benefits to be received when you have been freed to enjoy the total pleasures and gifts of a people being blessed by God!

*"And I will pray the Father, and he shall give you another Comforter, that he may abide with you for ever;*

*Even the Spirit of truth; whom the world cannot receive, because it seeth him not, neither knowest him: but ye know him; for he dwelleth with you, and shall be in you."*

*"I have yet many things to say unto you, but ye cannot bear them now.*

*Howbeit when he, the Spirit of truth, is come, he will guide you into all truth: for he shall not speak of himself; but whatsoever he shall hear, that shall he speak: and he will show you things to come."*

**St. John 14:16-17; 16:12-13**

Many sayings attributed to Yeshua (Jesus) allude to a relationship between hearing and understanding the message of God and the state of one's soul. Therefore, the Truth about the worship of God has to be pursued with all of one's heart, soul and might. You must seek it as water

110

when thirsty, as food when hungry. You must feel that you cannot live without it. A knowable Truth about the true God is that His worship is established upon Truth. Only an individual bereft of a mind could conclude that the worship of God, based upon a lie, could keep someone in harmony with God. If we do not serve God properly and represent His interests well, He will not shower down His blessings upon us. Thus, we can easily conclude that the predicament of humanity is a result of improper worship. Once you are made aware of this Truth, you will be born again. You must be reborn into a new world with a new spirit. When I say being reborn into a "new" world, don't conclude that this means dying and going to heaven (as prescribed in contemporary religion). By now, you should know that the "pie-in-the-sky-when-you-die" nonsense is just that - nonsense.

Being reborn also goes beyond the cries of "praise Jesus" after every joyous event. Those of you who already consider that you've been "reborn" when you "accepted Jesus Christ as your personal savior" are sadly mistaken also. Again, salvation and the new birth entails more than your ability to speak in tongues or how much you're tithing to your personal church home. You have to truly understand that no truly new birth is back into the same world, nor does the born again individual see or feel the same about the former world. When the spark of life or the shock (like electricity) of Truth ignites you, the once dormant spiritual energy will come alive, causing you to spring up to regain your senses. This new energy and new purpose will fill your life with daily activities on behalf of God.

Many professing to have been born again have been deceived or have deceived themselves. They can neither explain what they have become, nor do they accept the truth of what they were. Beyond the utterance of the obvious "I was a sinner" or "I've been born again out of sin", most people's rebirth actually only involves having been exposed to a new phrase; they are divorced from the significance of its true meaning. Truthfully, they've never been introduced to the fruit that a new birth is supposed to yield. If you are to understand these things written, you must base your conclusions on knowledge and wisdom instead of on in-vogue fronts and emotions. Remember, when people have been living a lie, it should be understandable that only the Truth can set them free.

Bear in mind that throughout history, people professing to be of God have compromised their faith with those who believed not, and thought to challenge God's authority. However, God controls everything. He is the shaper and molder of events that form history. Only God Almighty was able to set in motion the milestones we know as prophecy. What is history? History is a movement directed toward an end by God the Creator. His direction was revealed by the prophets and wise men of old. As true history is written, God will always be the central figure.

In recent years, the world has witnessed the unfolding of political events that have altered the course of all of our lives, not just those immediately involved in the occurrences, and changed history.

When the current deputy director of the U.S. State Department's policy planning staff wrote The End of History, he was revealing that a portion of the liberal democratic influences saw the fall or defeat of communism as an end. This did not mean the end of eastern bloc nations, but that the historical struggle between the two blocs had ended. That struggle would no longer have major historical significance. Allow me to elucidate.

Prior to the collapse of the communist bloc, the Euro-gentile/American government, media and others used the ideological differences of the capitalistic West and communist East to inspire valor, dedication and a sense of purpose and mission in the quest for the downfall and disposal of communism. Since the end of World War II, the Soviet Union (Russia) has been referred to as the "evil empire". New history has to now be written which will paint a completely different picture, while encouraging the coming generations to see the Soviet Union from the era of the Head of State, Mikael Gorbachev. This new history has to redirect the valor, dedication and sense of purpose and mission.

A single personality has dominated and played the major role in bringing about the end of East vs. West. This personality emerged in a regime that defied change. The man of the decade or century was not born in the liberal West but in the rigid East. In some circles, Mr.

Gorbachev is considered to have saved both the East and the West..a savior. This savior does not believe in God. Subsequently, should we rejoice or be highly suspicious of the ultimate destiny of this new allegiance? Somehow, a non-believing deliverer has been made a hero of a world of supposed believers.

We should therefore not be deceived into believing that a New World Order has begun. We who stand for God must not drop our guard.

This "end" is a deceptive end to turn our eyes and attention away from the end that shall come, after which things shall truthfully get better.

Another illustration of the crucial ties between history and the future can be seen in the history of African Americans. We as an African people committed the cardinal sin of allowing ourselves to be cut off from our history. Without our history, our present is dead. We are speedily moving toward an end that we cannot avoid or understand because we have been severed from our historical past. The present can only come alive when we remember the past. Only our historical Truth can give us the keys to avert extinction on this planet. To fail to understand, review, and simultaneously force our children to peruse our Biblical history has broken the chain of historical remembrances and denied us our true identity. Black children's true identity is found, in part, in a chain of people who are in a peculiar predicament because of the hand of God being set against them.[1] Wherever we of African descent are, our lives and countries are torn by strife, dissension and disunity. This flows into every level of society, including family.

It should have become evident that the systems of the so-called "New World" which have been superimposed upon Blacks do not hold the authoritative solutions to our problem. Thus, we grope as a blind man at noonday. We need a dynamic, historical awakening to lead us in a social revolution that will guide us to consummate joy and oneness with God. The success of our mission only requires that the Eternal One be pleased with us. To please God, we must first seek Biblical clarity. The primary source of Biblical clarity is the law and inspired writings of the prophets. If there is to be any Biblical journey, we must begin by

---

[1] (See "Introduction" to my first book, <u>God the Black Man and Truth.</u>)

acknowledging that these writings are a revelation of God. It is not my objective to categorize all other writings that were in circulation during the first through third centuries as Revelations of God. Yet, I will and must clarify your understanding concerning those writings by their relationship to the root from which they were supposedly born.

During the life of Yeshua (Jesus) and shortly thereafter, there was an abundance of writers and writings. These writings were not <u>necessarily</u> being inscribed as part of the Canon. For example, modern Biblical scholars have concluded that the books of the New Testament should be thus ordered: oldest author, Paul; letters attributed to him, Galatians and Romans, written between 50-64 C.E. Next is Mark, written in 70 C.E.; Matthew and Luke, 100 C.E.; and John, 120 C.E. Other first century groups circulating doctrinal writings were the Pharisees, Saducees, Samaritans, Essenes, Oumran Community, Apocalyptists, Zealots, Kasidim, Babylonian Hebrews, Egyptian Hebrews, Hellenistic Hebrews and Nazarenes. Much of the teachings of Yeshua (Jesus) of Nazareth were drawn from these sources of written information. It would be extremely misleading to conclude that every saying attributed to Yeshua (Jesus) was an introduction to a new doctrinal position. Furthermore, you must not be misled to believe that Yeshua (Jesus) was an opponent of the Hebrew Canon. For example, let us review the portion concerning the woman accused of adultery.

*"And the scribes and Pharisees brought unto him a woman taken in adultery; and when they had set her in the midst,*

*They say unto him, Master, this woman was taken in adultery, in the very act.*

*Now Moses in the law commanded us, that such should be stoned: but what sayest thou?*

*This they said, tempting him, that they might have to accuse him. But Jesus stooped down, and with his finger wrote on the ground, as though he heard them not."*

**St. John 8:3-6**

114

## Law, Knowable Truth and Spiritual Energy

*"And the man that committeth adultery with another man's wife, even he that committeth adultery with his neighbor's wife, the adulterer and the adulteress shall surely be put to death."*

**Leviticus 20:10**

We must discern an important point here. They were attempting to give the impression that Yeshua (Jesus) did not accept the law. This angered Yeshua (Jesus). Thus, the central focal point moved from the woman to those that were attempting to create a false image of him before the people. He thus responded by testing their own obedience to the law. He rebuked them not for bringing the woman but for attempting to create a division between himself and Moses. They that brought the woman drifted away, calling into question the legitimacy of their claim. Yeshua (Jesus) thus said, "Go and sin on more."

It would be a gross error to view that incident as the new relationship between the law and adultery, whereas those involved should just be told to "go and sin no more." Thus, the Truth prevails when accepted. If we can agree that Yeshua (Jesus) was an anointed Master Teacher, in that we may find our answer. No teacher, master or anointed of God would ever - could ever - create a framework for safe adultery.

Many people who say they believe in God and follow the Scriptures have been misled by an incorrect analysis of the Holy writings. As in the example above regarding adultery, as well as my point concerning animal sacrifices, entire societies and their philosophies for behavior have been governed by a misinterpreted exposition of the Biblical writings. With that in mind, I would like to touch upon another point known as dietary sanity and dietary insanity.

The great majority of the earth's inhabitants consume food as if it has nothing to do with their health. It is not my objective to detail the detestable items consumed by man today, but I will most definitely negate any Biblical justification for such irresponsibility.

*"If any man have ears to hear, let him hear.*

*And when he was entered into the house from the people, his disciples asked him concerning the parable.*

*And he saith unto them, Are ye so without understanding also? Do ye not perceive, that whatsoever thing from without entereth into the man, it cannot defile him;*

*Because it entereth not into his heart, but into the belly, and goeth out into the draught, purging all meats?*

*And he said, That which cometh out of the man, that defileth the man.*

*For from within, out of the heart of men, proceed evil thoughts, adulteries, fornications, murders,*

*Thefts, covetousness, wickedness, deceit, lasciviousness, an evil eye, blasphemy, pride, foolishness:*

*All these evil things come from within, and defile the man."*

**St. Mark 7:16-23**

The Bible from Genesis has guided us in the direction of dietary consciousness. And even if you are not a student of the Bible, by now you should be aware that there are dietary customs that will inevitably bring about disease, and on the other hand, there are dietary habits that are not conducive to the proliferation of disease. Does this sound strange? Good health is relative to a good diet, but what is a good diet? That depends upon the objective of whoever is controlling the Power to Define. (See "Power to Define" chapter, God the Black Man and Truth.) Remember, you don't live in a world that protects its citizens from dangerous, anti-health substances but one which authorizes their sale although, after being exposed, the manufacturers do alter them slightly from time to time. Yeshua (Jesus) reminded us that whatever line of thought is received into the consciousness goes on working until it is rooted out by another line of thinking, or until it changes one's whole consciousness in every aspect and manifests fully in his outer life expressions. Thus Yeshua (Jesus) admonishes us not to direct our energies to what a man eats, but what he thinks. The layout of his table is not the problem; the layout of his mind is. If someone is eating a forbidden food and you seek a solution to the problem by hiding the supply, or maybe you even go further by discontinuing the production and he still desires to eat it, then the sin is still upon him. He is still as one who eats forbidden foods - in his mind.

It is the spirit that quickeneth; the flesh profiteth nothing. If he never desired to eat the forbidden food, the dish itself would not bother him. It was the thought or the lust that defiled him, or that is/was the source of the problem. Yeshua (Jesus) was definitely not advocating an end to the consecration of man's diet. No true Messenger of God will ever support a position of unrestrained consumption of food. As a matter of historical Truth, all teachers, masters or anointed of God have as a part of their message, dietary restraint and discipline. No one of a sane mind could insinuate or teach that Yeshua (Jesus) ate swine flesh. Anyone teaching that Yeshua (Jesus) ate or would condone the eating of swine has to be confuted. This person has not been moved by the Spirit of Truth by the true and living God. He is neither a teacher, master nor anointed of God. If at any time these things which I have written are displeasing to you, know that they are not born out of hostility, but Truth; not to weaken your faith, but to rekindle your faith; not to take Yeshua (Jesus) away from you, (for Euro-gentile, Euro-centric theology accomplished that), but to bring you back unto Him.

I am trying to reconnect you with the real historical Jesus. The fact is that the Yeshua (Jesus) believed in, portrayed and spoken of today isn't consanguineous with the Yeshua (Jesus) of the Bible. No one can truly believe in Yeshua (Jesus) except that they believe in the law and the testimony of the prophets of God. Any scholar who loves the New Testament has to first love the Old Testament. No one can believe in the New Canon and offer scepticism of the Old Canon. Yeshua (Jesus) instructed: "Search the scriptures [Old Testament Canon was the only accepted revelation of God at the time these words were spoken] for in them ye think ye have eternal life. And they are they which testify of me."

To deny the Old Testament is to deny that there ever was a man called Yeshua (Jesus). The New Testament only exists through the truth of the words spoken by the prophets of God. Therefore, the onus is on New Testament believers to ascertain the truth and authenticity of the Old Testament and to maintain its legitimacy at all costs. If there appears to be something in the New Testament that comes into conflict with the older canon, it is the New Testament believer that has to be extremely careful of his position. If the foundation fails, the house will not stand. The servant does not surpass the Master, nor the created the Creator. You cannot afford to disqualify the law and testimony of the inspired prophets of God.

> *"Shall the axe boast itself against him that hewest therewith? Or shall the saw magnify itself against him that shaketh it? As if the rod should shake itself against them that lift it up, or as if the staff would lift up itself, as if it were no wood."*
>
> **Isaiah 10:15**

> *"And if a kingdom be divided against itself, that kingdom cannot stand.*
>
> *And if a house be divided against itself, that house cannot stand.*
>
> *And if Satan rise up against himself, and be divided, he cannot stand, but hath an end."*
>
> **St. Mark 3:24-26**

Now little children, you should be free of misleading restraints and the destructive harness that prohibits you from strengthening your relationship with God. If there is a New Testament scriptural reference that you have translated or that someone has defined for you, in which it supposedly says that you may now consume swine flesh, you my freely discard that scripture. If you trust that individual (author) to be an inspired teacher and you feel the need to defend him, then either the verses are being mistranslated (because he could not have meant that), or he did not write those verses. They were simply added by another author during the editing process. (Many additions were written in during the editing process during the formation of the New Testament Canon; in the case of Paul, whole epistles were added under his name.) The spiritual law of God which is to govern human conduct is absolute in the consciousness of Right and Truth. Within this sphere there is

118

room for flexibility (within Right), change (Right), adaptation (Right), and amendment (Right).

From Genesis to the departure of the Children of Israel from Egypt under Moses, the diet underwent a significant transition and now in the days of the Kingdom of God, we have arrived back to a dietary genesis. Nevertheless, during no period of this transition has man ever been Biblically authorized to consume swine flesh. The swine has the dubious, rare Biblical distinction of being a beast whose dead carcass was forbidden to be touched by human hand. Only an adversary of God would, in turn, make this beast the pride of the Euro-centric and African American diets. My/these explanations of Truth about certain elements of Yeshua's (Jesus') teachings or your traditional beliefs are not an attempt to weaken, but to strengthen your relationship with God. Where I have had to challenge traditional beliefs, it has not been with any hostile intent. On the contrary, it is to fortify your faith in God and to give you the necessary strength to cast off the heavy burden of destructive lies.

> *"Do not think that I will accuse you to the Father; there is one that accuseth you, even Moses, in whom ye trust.*
>
> *For had ye believed Moses, ye would have believed me: for he wrote of me.*
>
> *But if ye believe not his writings, how shall ye believe my words?"*
>
> **St. John 5:45-47**

My objective is to put a right spirit back into the world and to bring humanity back to life again. With the help and inspiration of God, I am breathing Truth upon them to revive their comatose souls. Humanity, under the control of Err, is easily mis-directed and controlled. They are inert on the vital issues affecting their lives. For example, they know from the depths of their souls that politicians are the greatest threat to the continued existence of life on this planet. They seem to want a change. The spirit seems willing, but the flesh is inept. These things are hidden from the power elite and revealed unto babes. Salvation will come from the last, not the first, in this world. The momentum has to start at the bottom and carry the outcasts of societies to the top to save this planet earth.

In the midst of great political opposition, the poor and needy will soon become redeemers and saviors of humanity. The "first" will be the last to positively respond to the Word of God and the "last" will be first. Strangely enough, the rich are not genuinely disturbed by what they do; it is the poor that are distraught at what they see being done.

*"But many that are first shall be last; and the last shall be first."*

**St. Matthew 19:30**

*"Rejoice greatly, O daughter of Zion: shout, O daughter of Jerusalem: behold, thy King cometh unto thee: he is just, and having salvation; Lowly, and riding upon an ass, and upon a colt the foal of an ass."*

**Zechariah 9:9**

*"And he showed me Joshua the high priest standing before the angel of the Lord, and Satan standing at his right hand to resist him.*

*And the Lord said unto Satan, the Lord rebuke thee, O Satan: even the Lord that hath chosen Jerusalem rebuke thee. Is not this a brand plucked out of the fire?*

*Now Joshua was clothed with filthy garments, and stood before the angel.*

*And he answered and spoke unto those that stood before him, saying, Take away the filthy garments from him. And unto him he said, Behold, I have caused thine iniquity to pass from thee, and I will clothe thee with change of raiment.*

*And I said, Let them set a fair mitre upon his head. So they set a fair mitre upon his head, and clothed him with garments, and the angel of the Lord stood by.*

*And the angel of the Lord protested unto Joshua, saying,*

*Thus saith the Lord of hosts; If thou wilt walk in my ways, and if thou wilt keep my charge, then thou shalt also judge my house, and shalt also keep my courts, and I will give thee places to walk among these that stand by."*

**Zechariah 3:1-7**

*"And it shall come to pass in that day, that the Lord shall beat off from the channel of the river unto the stream of Egypt, and ye shall be gathered one by one, O ye children of Israel.*

*And it shall come to pass in that day, that the great trumpet shall be blown, and they shall come which are ready to perish in the land of Assyria, and the outcasts in the land of Egypt, and shall worship the Lord in the holy mount at Jerusalem."*

**Isaiah 27:12-13**

In Zechariah, the mention of the kingly, Messianic spirit coming riding upon an ass and a foal (young ass) born from she-asses (more than one), literally means that a gospel will come forth from the mouths of, on the backs of, or with the support of the lowly and meek of the people, not the high and the mighty. The Deliverer will champion the cause of both young and old, male and female. He will be truthful and just. He will take up the issues that weigh heavy, that are significant and important to the poor in flesh and spirit and give solutions that are in harmony with the will of God.

The street language of "he's riding high" (in the worldly sense) simply means that he's "all inside" the system; he is committed to success in evil. The opposite to that would be riding low or lowly, or not "all inside", still possessing some basic insight into what is good and right. It is from the midst of that lowly segment of society that the Deliverer will spring forth. He will emerge from amongst those considered left out or dropouts - those appearing to be insignificant.

For centuries, beleaguered souls have cried out unto God to send a Savior. We may cite some historical examples. First, in the Deliverance of Israel from Egypt, there was strong resistance to Moses from those riding high in Egypt - those feeling that they had succeeded in Egypt.

They felt that Egypt was as much theirs as the Egyptians. Their most common reply was "we built Egypt". But the majority of support for Moses came from the lowly; those having to make bricks without straw or perform the menial and simple jobs. (Not all of the Israelites were literally making bricks. See Exodus 1:7.) Coupled with the metaphor of the poor and lowly is the image of the ass which is known as the beast of burden, upon whom the hardest tasks are put and to whom the least in compensation for his labours is given. Who would you consider the ass of American and European civilization? If you answered the African American (also known as coon, buck, nigger, jungle bunny, sambo, pickaninny), you are correct. Furthermore, just as Yeshua (Jesus) was a layman - a carpenter by profession - who God anointed as the Savior, the much talked about and long-awaited Messiah or Deliverer will emerge from the midst of those called African Americans in America, the land of their chastisement.

We also find in the return of the people under Ezra and Nehemiah further evidence to support that Deliverers are/were mainly accompanied by the supposedly poor and unlearned. Again we recall that Yeshua (Jesus) of Nazareth also faced fierce opposition from the wealthy and learned Hebrew Israelites. They identified with the oppressors, the Roman tyrants, although their authority was only over the Israelites. They were not charged with authority over Romans in any real sense. Even today, we find that those African Americans in positions of influence do not support African Americans returning to reclaim our land, language and culture, our very souls.

The history and culture of the African American transcends the boundaries of West Africa, the shackles of the American slavery era and the pages of Roots. Our history is truly a unique, peculiar epoch that once fully known, will explain the peculiarity of Black peoples "hidden" heritage and more importantly, the special relationship Blacks have with God. Despite the extraordinary obstacles that have obscured the acceptance of Blacks, there remains an unquestionable faith and belief in God. Encompassed in the return of African Americans from exile, is, more importantly, the reconciliation with our God and our people. Following a sacred and Holy way of life is the surest path to reconciliation with God. Without that "way of life", what would be your sanctifier?

What would make you a "peculiar" or "special people"? We must also consider that if our "way of life" will make us different from the entire world, then theirs must be a "way of death"!

The reaction to Truth is characterized all too often by an attack on the messenger and no serious consideration of the critical message. This propensity is supercharged by fear of change and/or having to admit to a lifestyle of error. We see a similar reaction from the well-entrenched opponents of Yeshua (Jesus) who feared to venture into the world of his words. However, the truth is that the synergism would have greatly enhanced their own position in the midst of the people. Their communities and numbers far outnumbered those of Yeshua (Jesus).

Sometimes when an individual plans the way he wants to be saved, he ends up rejecting the way God wants to save him. This is the scenario in Euro-American, European theology. It purposely proliferates a plan of redemption that will never come to pass and depicts an image of a savior that will never come. When the blind lead the blind, they both fall into the pit. Is there an escape from or an end to the habitation of man that has been made a hell on earth? To escape the horrible fate of a world trying to avoid living under the rule and authority of God, man's eyes will have to be opened to a new vision. He must submit unto the will of God, for only with the shield of Truth can he ward off all of the fiery darts of the wicked. This - the struggle that will end all struggles - is not against flesh and blood, but against high officials, those in power who control the destinies of men; governors of this world who are also the perpetuators of spiritual wickedness in high places.

This is the hour of decision and, as is often the case, the right decision seems hardest and not immediately the most popular one to make. The Epistle of Peter outlines our mission: The heavens (minds) in uproar (confusion, ruins) must pass away and the elements (fundamentals, rudiments, foundations) must melt from fervent heat; the earth, with the works that are upon it, must be burned up." The ineptness of man to rise to this historical challenge is the result of years of subtle training by the power elite (angels of darkness) disguised as educators, the clergy and the media, or as I prefer to call them, "messengers of light". It will not be easy to "unlearn" the misconceptions and bad habits acquired during that time. When man opted for financial security, the price he paid was the discarding of many of the keys to the essential chambers of survival. After his extensive imprisonment, he has adjusted to darkness; the slightest light (Truth, wisdom, enlightenment) causes fear and discomfort. He has become animalistic; his mind is in ruin. How was the victim to know he had befriended a hostile "element"? And, as if in a chapter out of a science-fiction novel, the "element" turned against him and took control of his planet earth.

# Chapter VI

# The Elements

## *(Shall Melt From Intensive Heat)*

### "*ELEMENT*"

"One of the four substances, air, water, fire and earth, formerly believed to compose the physical universe, weather conditions, caused by the activity of the elements, especially violent or severe weather. The state or sphere natural or suited to a person or thing. The example here is: ...at school she was in her "element". A constituent part, as the simplest principles of a subject of study; rudiments. One of a number of distinct groups composing a human community (the criminal "element" in the city); one of the necessary data or values on which calculations or conclusions are based; one of the factors determining the outcome of a process. Synonyms; component, constituent, ingredient; one of the parts, substances, or principles that make up a compound or complex whole."

**(Webster's New Collegiate Dictionary 1981)**

If you seriously consider this definition, it is almost unnecessary to elucidate further. Nevertheless, so there will be no room for error, I must elaborate. Elements affect the physical universe and weather. Thus, if there is a hostile element attempting to destroy the physical universe, it would be the source of destruction of air, water, fire and earth, or in contemporary terminology, the environment. It would destroy the ozone which would have a negative effect on the sun's ultra-violet rays (fire), thereby altering weather patterns and causing natural disasters and destruction.

These elements make up the physical universe. If they are defeated, man becomes extinct. Hell was created by the presence of certain evil elements. In the beginning there was no hell. These elements are now

125

so prolific until they appear normal. Evil elements now govern every facet of man's life. They have been so meticulously woven into man's lifestyle until he now actually depends on them to exist. There are very few elders remaining who can tell the younger generations how things once were. In another ten to twenty years, there will be only the generations of the damned, those that were born and raised by parents that know only this illusion. Therefore, they would say unto God, "Depart from us, for we desire not the knowledge of Thy ways. Who is God Almighty, that we should serve him? What more can we profit by praying to Him?" Maybe even at this very moment these words have been echoing in your ears. The opposition to evil has almost been silenced. Hell on earth, not beneath the earth, has become the natural dwelling place for the vast majority of the earth's people and they love it.

Returning to the definition of element, allow me to elaborate on the portion of the definition that concerns "one of the distinct groups composing a human community." Let us consider some of the elements within society that must be destroyed, according to the vision of Peter. Today's average family as well as the typical male/female element within the community is actually the element I consider tantamount to hell on earth in which we find men afraid to be overly masculine and women preferring to assume the role of men. Children can take parents to court, decide on sex and abortions legally without the parents' consent. In the Euro-American feminist movement, the catchword has become "equality". In practice, this equality has become suspiciously synonymous with "sameness". Women in broad-shouldered business suits or as contorting weight lifters epitomize how women have begun to look and act like men. The evil element's goal is to create a genderless society and completely interchangeable roles. For all intents and purposes, the feminist movement has removed all traces of feminity and now the new world must create women again, in the image and likeness of God.

David prayed unto God: "Lead me in the cycles of righteousness for thy namesake." In the life cycle there are proper roles for men, women and children. They should never have been altered, or should we say, violated. Proper cycles simply mean that in this sphere, the right things will develop and be developed. Somehow, in the infinite plan of God, obedience to this plan kept us in a realm called "the everlasting". To violate this order halted human development and brought in a cycle of time called confusion.

No man can truthfully play the role of a woman. Nor is a woman created to mentally or physically be cast into the function of a man. When right cycles are broken, both physical and mental decay sets in. The wrong cause will only yield the wrong effects. As a result of violation of the ordinances of God, the family is in a state of decay. If that is not bad enough, so are each of the individual members - men, women and children. They are out of cycle and totally confused, possessed by an evil element. As a starter, a re-defining by Godly definers of what constitutes a family is desperately needed. It is out-rageous to include or legalize live-in lovers or homosexuals as families and thus give intellectual credibility to this type of confusion as experts have done in America. Doing so has not and will not work or solve the problems in the African American and human family. They have only compounded the problem by equating the misnomers "live-in" or homosexual mates with family. The problem is the failure to structure families and societies based on Truth, a sense of respect and account-ability to the laws governing the cycles of life. Solomon stated, "seek wisdom and knowledge, but above all things, get thee an understanding."

Within the cycles of right, both men and women have been given sense to guide them in day-to-day living in a relationship of love of God and each other. They, at times, do special things for each other. Then there are times that call for something beyond the call of duty, when men will change the diapers, handle the wash, serve his wife breakfast in bed, take the baby for a walk, mop the floor, clean the house and even handle the shopping. Some of these things can be somewhat amusing and fun while bringing mutual pleasure and probably lots of laughter. Nevertheless, you must make a difference between doing things to offer needed assistance and doing them as a continuous action or your "role" in the family. Many of the above-mentioned require the continuous action of a female. No man can provide that necessity and remain of sound masculine character. This is why we find that a righteous society will have laws that systematically call for community living and community concern to structure and oversee the roles within the home. A God-inspired lifestyle automatically brings with it brotherhood and sisterhood. A situation developing that requires a man to strap the baby on his front or back or grab the stroller is not a sin or violation of the ordinances of God. But as a continuous action, the presence of a woman is required for the sake of the family, the children, husband, wife, community and nation. It will prevent the development of perverted idealism and perverted people, thus inevitably becoming sin. In order for the proper roles of the man and woman to be maintained, in the absence of a woman, either the family, the community or nation has to provide assistance.

It is not within the righteous nature of a man to provide continuous action that is of a feminine disposition. There is more involved in raising toddlers, washing diapers and preparing meals than what meets the carnal eye. There is a mood, a temperament and behavior that is essential and has to accompany all role models for both men and women. If an individual is cast out of cycle on a continuous basis, perversion is inevitable. We need not debate...only watch. Let us briefly review the contemporary movie industry's portrayal of male and female roles. Men are being cast as cowardly, sex-hungry squirrels, crying on screen like babies while the woman slaps his face and instructs him to "Get a hold of yourself!" Women are more and more the image of strength while men succumb to weak rabbit roles. Then there are a few men being cast as super heroes. Yet, they don't come off in their roles as manly men but as perverted strong men. Their screen dress and makeup reveals a feminine kind of strength. Something is missing. There are elements that make men always appear as men; they cried like men and they died like men. Without that element they can't act like men.

Next, we find the political and social elements. Politicians are highly-skilled, professional liars. No one believes politicians. What is being asked and debated now is whether it is even possible for a politician to tell the truth. The political element is used to keep a protective shield around the corruption and corruptors of this earth. The facets of power they control are the arenas they attend for participating in life control and manipulation. They must assure the protection of evil's freedom. Politicians love the hell they have created. The fire doesn't seem to bother them; the hotter, the better. Gays and homosexuals are normal citizens that are allowed to be legally married and live happy lives. The politician is said to be of the people, for the people, and by the people..the people that house cars but evict people from their homes; that bake genital-shaped sweets from dough; that dance the "butt" and "freak"; that accept homosexuals as normal; that boast of millionaires and billionaires, hungry and homeless. Politicians attend church on Sunday and mourn for those killed by violence. They attend movies and clap enthusiastically at the violence on the screen, which influences the violence in the streets. Theirs is the dependable constituency that is a part of the complex whole. They continuously elect and select the right officials to do the wrong things. Their role is to listen and observe carefully so that no right (righteous) element gets their support. Unfortunately, they have the people's power, but instead of the real power for the right people, the results of feigned "progress" have been devastating. In the case of the African Americans' participation in the political system, the bottom line is that they are allowed to participate in the very system that is the source of their misery. Consequently, this double indemnity brought about the development of a suitable state of mind that has to defend the system on the one hand, and to victimize the same people being represented on the other. In addition, the African American politician had to also agree to be the victim when necessary, without extreme reaction. Thus, through a process called "success", the people are neutralized and become unfruitful. They all become little personal islands. Their primary concern is now self-preservation as defined by the very system that is actually their enemy.

The problem is that you have yet to realize the things you are in search of can only be found in something you do not have...freedom. Deceptive education and deceptive leaders neutralized your freedom struggle. You attained knowledge but were unskilled in the proper use of knowledge. To know is not to be wise, for there is no fool so great as the knowing fool. But the correct use of knowledge equals wisdom - the gift of God. The end result of your training is to qualify you to attain a job. Profit becomes the trend. You are employed; you feel a sense of security (as you were taught). The next illusion is "Now I can begin to enjoy life a little." Now you begin using your "purchasing power", as it is called, instead of debt accumulation or a credit trap. Therefore, you spend your earnings to strengthen those who control the system which you were initially struggling against. Then you attend the monthly freedom meeting and you constantly are bombarded with the complaint that African Americans are not financially supporting African American organizations. You're shocked; you want to contribute. But you're broke. You're donating everything to the structure that you were told is the opposition. You return home feeling something has to be done, but then subliminal deception reminds you that "you risk losing all of the gains you've made if you get too involved."

The plan has worked again as he equated: Education = Job = Security = Gains = Living = Demobilization. You soon lose your ability to see with your eyes and hear with your ears. At that stage of your underdevelopment, you sit before the television daily viewing the news concerning your plight being broadcast to Euro-American viewers. They assure them that things for you are getting worse, so they can relax. After the broadcast, you open up your refrigerator and enjoy another beer, not having heard or seen anything that aroused your interest; after all, they weren't talking about you.

If you were convinced of a chasm between you and God as being the problem, would you make such a momentous effort to get back inside or to become integrated into His lifestyle as you have in attempting to integrate and become an active part of the American dream? Let me put it this way. If the African American would try as hard to please God as he has to please man, in one decade he would become the light of the world. But "if the salt loses its savour, wherein shalt it season? It is good for nothing except to be cast out and trodden under the foot of man." (St. Matthew 5:13-16)

Would the African American undergo similar hardships on a path leading back unto God? Would he consider a "God-struggle? I am convinced that it would be easier, but again, the power of deception comes into play. If you saw a people paying the kind of price you're paying in returning to God, you would call them crazy and probably proclaim them to be following a madman. Yet, the statistics do not justify your ultimate objective.

# The Messiah and the End of this World

Why have we sacrificed so many tens of thousands and so many generations of youth, dignity and reason for an objective of acquiring materialistic accoutrements and token integration? Truthfully, it appears that you are crazy and following a madman. Can you imagine a nation going to war for a cause like that? Does it sound somewhat embarrassing? It should! Yours is an unworthy struggle, unworthy of the title "struggle". It is no wonder then as to why we are laughed at by other revolutionaries. We have been experimenting with what others can do for us for over 400 years. Now we survey the landscape of the broken homes and hearts, disease compounded and strength lost. We conclude: all they can do for us is to destroy us.

We/you will have to forsake the family of the flesh to find the everlasting family of the spirit. For the flesh profits nothing; the spirit does revive.

*"But let him ask in faith, nothing wavering. For he that wavereth is like a wave of the sea driven with the wind and tossed.*

*For let not that man think that he shall receive anything of the Lord.*

*A double minded man is unstable in all his ways."*

**James 1:6-8**

*"For if God spared not the angels that sinned, but cast them down to hell, and delivered them into chains of darkness, to be reserved unto judgment;*

*And spared not the old world, but saved Noah the eighth person, a preacher of righteousness, bringing in the flood upon the world of the ungodly;*

*And turning the cities of Sodom and Gomorrah into ashes condemned them with an overthrow, making them an example unto those that after should live ungodly;*

*And delivered just Lot, vexed with the filthy conversation of the wicked.*

131

## The Elements (Shall Melt from Intensive Heat)

*(For that righteous man dwelling among them, in seeing and hearing, vexed his righteous soul from day to day with their unlawful deeds;)"*

**II Peter 2:4-8**

You need the motivation of a Savior; you need to reach out for the Kingdom of God, a society based on the precepts of righteousness, justice and equality which emanates the presence of God and serves as the living example for all men. This is a society where solutions to seemingly irreversible problems that plague mankind are being found and put into practice. As the 20th century comes to a close, we are the ones who have come to realize that the pursuit of the modern technological society is not the answer to that which ails man. For this reason we have sacrificed our individual interests and invested our lives in the building of the Kingdom of God on earth, a viable solution for the salvation of all men. If all men worshipped God properly, there would be no hole in the ozone, the water would be safe to drink, there would never again be a threat of war and there would be no inequality among men.

Let us continue our perusal of the elements that must be burned up. "One of the necessary data or values on which calculations or conclusions are based; "one of the factors determining the outcome of a process." That means that there is a sequence of events that leads to an inevitable conclusion. To promote alcoholic beverages as denoting high-class increases the consumption amongst the poor. Because of the relatively poor diet of the underprivileged, liver infections will spread fast but alcohol will be blamed less. Because of their "values", they will complain less (you've got to die for something). Complaining less means better acceptance, less guilt. Less guilt encourages bolder seduction, which increases sales through an illusion of innocence. As the old saying goes, "If you play your hand bad, you make the cards run bad." As with pests, after years of continuous spraying with destructive poison, they adjust and develop what seems to be an immunity; they become stronger and even more ferocious consumers. They thus consume the pesticides and continue the process of destruction. They become immune to evil; it becomes their natural habitat...within or surrounded by that which was once intended to kill. Soon the symptoms of over-consumption of alcohol will take longer to detect, encouraging them to drink even more, allowing for even greater proliferation of alcohol and a large increase in alcoholics.

The evil element has built an entire infrastructure as a result of the low values of large portions of their populations. These industries are geared toward maintaining the low value the people place upon themselves. If their values change, these companies go under. The collapse of these enterprises would affect jobs, taxes and government stability. Thus, someone "calculates" and "draws conclusions". The plan of containment and destruction is working effectively. It is essential to Euro-American society that the African American maintains a very low moral value. By this alone, they can calculate his strengths and weaknesses, his present direction and ultimate destiny. Black America is 400 years behind, certainly not by choice but by purposeful intention, to keep us, the former standard-bearers of God, from ever regaining our rightful places as leaders in a new world.

I quote from my writing, God the Black Man and Truth, page 155, paragraphs two and three:

"We were disconnected from our very soul. We became a non-people seeking to be every race except our own. We were totally de-Africanized. This was necessary for the survival of white America's superiority, because their superiority is established upon a weak foundation that cannot stand challenge or comparison. Certainly, they could not stand the competition of great African minds and institutions. Therefore, through their educational system, whites had to systematically destroy Africa. There could be no association or knowledge of past greatness.

As an African, the slave was forced into the back door; as a negro, he walked out of the front door, willingly giving credit unto his master. Unfortunately, he never saw the neon sign blinking overhead that read "What has a man gaineth if he gaineth the whole world and loses his soul?" The oppressor listened to the playback of his product. It was a job well done, for now negroes spoke a strange language announcing "I ain't no African", "I ain't lost nothing in Africa"; "Those people eat one another"; "I'm proud to be a negro." In the era

133

of the negro, which brought with it the period of submission, self-alienation and self-contempt, the soul of the African was doomed."

These are some of the factors that have been determining the outcome of the process. The outcome leaves a people playing a happy role in a very unpleasant situation, seeing no internal hope, yet afraid to pursue an external dream, willingly accepting the crumbs instead of at least making an effort to attain the loaf. The intellectuals in control of the data banks, positions of power and wealth are aware of and in perfect agreement with the purposeful exploitation of the wretched of God's earth, and have skillfully hidden those things from their conscious minds. Whereas in the days of the Kingdom of God, the heavenly Father will avenge their exploitation by hiding His Truths from the high and mighty and reveal them instead unto babes, the meek and weak (relatively) of the earth that shall confound and dumbfound the power brokers of today. It is the high and the mighty that must come down that those considered lowly may take them up into the new world - Heaven and Earth.

We receive a lesson in this from the story of Lazarus and the rich man. We take note that at the end of his term as a beggar at the rich man's table, Lazarus became the one sought after by the rich man to ease his torment. The poor man was taken by angels to a higher dwelling place and comforted by the spirits of the fathers, in whose faith he had continued. He was comforted by the testimony of their truth being confirmed as the revelation of God. The rich man was trapped in a state of the non-repentant; he had enjoyed his wealth until the transition without change, remorse or repentance. Those individuals that remain dedicated to this world beyond a certain cycle of time become trapped outside of the realm of salvation. In other words, they enjoy their evil until the end and after the transition, they are now ready to convert and partake of the New World. He had allowed too much time to lapse without reconciliation. This is thus defined to mean that he preferred evil over good, darkness instead of light. When the gulf is too wide, he can't cross over, nor be brought over into the New World.

As I have taught you before, this is judgment day, the day of the Lord. It is during this season you must repent, then renounce and break your allegiance to this society governed by men whose only interest is money and power, not lives and peace. I cannot tell you the day and time each individual season will end that brings us closer and closer to "the end". But each day the gulf gets wider and wider. Whereby you can save yourself and your family from the "mother of all wars". Be assured that you will not enjoy the New World except you deny this world in your conscious lifetime. The rich man then requested that Lazarus be sent back to warn his family of the widening bridge and again he was told as I have been telling you throughout your study. It is Moses and the inspired prophets of God that must be heard. Now because of evil elements, man has changed the Truth of God for a lie and works for and serves the manufactured more than the Creator. Man's mode of reasoning is senseless, without natural affection and implacable, giving consent to things opposed by God. Today's intellects are masters of all of the vile elements: the dietary element , the musical and dance element (heavy sound that drives children crazy or into devil worship rituals) the movie and video element, the religious element, the economic element, the obvious criminal element and the medical element. It was the medical element that initially influenced my dietary transition. Allow me to share an anecdote with you.

I was deeply moved by the heroism of men studying to be doctors, studying something that was going to cause them so much unhappiness. I concluded that the least I could do was to attempt to alleviate some of their suffering. It was partly for that reason that I became a vegetarian and tried to convince others to do the same. After succeeding as a vegan, I decided to start visiting doctors' offices to share the good news. I prepared myself with prayer and meditation for the period of wailing, moaning and lamenting I expected with each visit with these very unhappy, yet dedicated heroes. I set out on my journey and quite to my amazement...the doctors were not unhappy at all. I assumed there had to be some mistake; they seemed so happy and pleased. The more the clients, the happier they were. I, being somewhat naive, reasoned that those clients packing their offices probably were not sick constituents. While accompanying some of the doctors to their banks, I inquired: Do doctors treat the sick also? Their response was always the same: "All doctors' clients are sick." But if they are sick, I again reasoned, why are doctors happy instead of sad? It is because they are possessed by an evil element. In the world to come, it will be the absolute objective of every surgeon, dentist and medical specialist to do away with the very need for himself (his practice). On the other hand, if we, whom the body serves and to whom it belongs, don't do the things necessary to protect our health, we encourage its loss. For in the final analysis, those of us who take responsibility for our own health will come out on top. It is time for those that know Truth to take the initiative and move expediently to communicate God's way of life to all of the earth's inhabitants.

In our review of the destructive elements, we certainly must not leave out the educational and industrial elements. To build a new world, we must begin to build a new thought pattern. The world of tomorrow will not resemble the world of today. Your present thought patterns were created in Euro-gentile educational institutions to perpetuate the dreams or nightmares of their founding fathers. In order to be saved from further destruction, man must submit to a process of re-education and re-dedication because he has existed in a world he created for himself without the guidance of God. Thus, man has fallen victim to his own ways and understanding. The very things he has been taught to do to enhance and prolong his life are destroying him. When he adapted a lifestyle which supposedly emulated living, he was in fact dying. When we open our eyes and truthfully examine almost any facet of today's modern society, we readily and plainly see how lost we have become in our search for a place. When man possessed the original "God-Mind", his thoughts were continuously to do good to and for one another. You were the caretaker of God's creation. Your creativity was Holy; your inventions were Godly. Your meat was the fruit of the trees. You loved the herbs of the field. You shared with and loved your brother; you knew and treasured the value of life and the pleasure of people.

Man, through deceptive education, has been given the impression that the earth is not his ultimate dwelling place. Therefore, he is complacent in watching all things around him being destroyed, while truthfully, there will be no journey to another planet. Man's inheritance is the earth; the earth only needs to be properly governed. Man boasts of an undefined freedom, whereas purposeless freedom is the problem. Man needs urgent restraints placed upon his destructive habits of freedom. It is for that reason that we are keen to define our freedom, for true freedom begins with discipline.

> *"For the very true beginning of her is the desire of discipline; and the care of discipline is love;*
>
> *And love is the keeping of her laws; and the giving heed unto her laws is the assurance of incorruption;*
>
> *And incorruption maketh us near unto God:*
>
> *Therefore the desire of wisdom bringeth to a kingdom."*

**The Apocrypha - Wisdom of Solomon 6:17-20**

We are free to live in harmony with and according to the will of God. Disciplined freedom does not infer license to commit evil but a responsibility to fellowman and God. The farmer is too free in his pursuit of yield; the scientist in his pursuit of inventions; the doctor in his pursuit of stature and antibiotic health care; the lawyer in his pursuit of conviction or acquittal; the educator in his pursuit of progress; and the industrialist is unscrupulously, mischievously and dangerously free in his pursuit of profit. Maybe the Big Brother of 1984 was really industry instead of government. Somehow it seems that industry has penetrated the sub-conscious of man and caused even more damage than religion. It is industry that has been at the forefront of the creation of lustful appetites and the worship of inanimate materialism. Industrialists portray their products as household gods. The idea conveyed is that the solution to all household problems can be found in some product being marketed.

Industry has taken the planet from man and imprisoned him within her walls. However, the present situation is either - or. Either we dismantle the present industrial complex or it will destroy us. We must return from excess to essential. Better that we lose our jobs than our lives.

> *"Evil shall slay the wicked; and they that hate the righteous shall be desolate.*

**Psalms 34:21**

# The Elements (Shall Melt from Intensive Heat)

*"For the Lord loveth judgment, and forsaketh not his saints; they are preserved for ever: but the seed of the wicked shall be cut off."*

**Psalms 37:28**

Isaiah the Prophet pleaded, "Come now, let us reason together." Let us weigh without preconceived conclusions. First, never expect the euphoria over a good idea to come from those who stand to lose by its acceptance. A house divided cannot stand strong pressure. There are those who will very skillfully take the solution and make it the problem.

A single culture dominates the human family as never before, yet you say the problem is still somewhat nebulous. If the world is to live, then it is evident that Europe and Euro-Americans must relinquish their roles as its leaders. Europe has imposed its inability to govern on the human family. Its inability to function within the cycles of life has caused havoc on this planet. No country, state or city has escaped the misjudgment of Europeans, yet most people continue to ride on the merry-go-round of false security and moral corruption. From moral corruption there is no cure except to be born again (dead to Euro-American, European society) - born to the new reasoning of God.

Let us consider automobiles as a mode of transportation. Automobiles are not evil; they merely need a righteous element to govern them. It is the Euro-mental element that has turned a usable product into a curse. Automobiles must be put into a cycle of a metal machine used to move man and goods from one point to another. It does not dictate life or living, elevated or cast down. We must have our eyes opened to this fact. After removing the practice of measuring the stature of a human from the vehicle, we will be free to use it properly and not be used by it. It will not make our friends for us or our enemies. We can live without it or skillfully use it. It is the Euro-element that posts a safe speed limit, then sells you a vehicle that will travel three times faster than safely allowed. The same element warns you that "speed kills" and has sold you a vehicle that encourages speed as challenging and fun. It is the same element that issues you your speeding ticket or your coffin.

The world to come will not be a world without automobiles, washing machines, television and other household appliances. There is no need for anxiety about washing on the scrub board. You must be re-educated concerning the Truth of materialism's value. We must transform you that you may transform these objects back into inanimate convenience and remove them from the list of items esteemed above your fellowman and worshipped. The world has to change to go into the new genesis and so will you. In the past you've stood up for what you believed. Now you must stand for what is right.

The Kingdom of God is the most serious and only viable alternative to world destruction. With the return of the sons and daughters of God, the earth is going to become beautiful again, as God returns to dominate our thinking, dominate our countries and guide our future. Let us join hands and hasten the New Heavens and the New Earth wherein Righteousness does reign.

*"Therefore shall the Lord, the Lord of hosts, send among his fat ones, leanness; and under his glory he shall kindle a burning like the burning of a fire.*

*And the light of Israel shall be for a fire, and his Holy One for a flame; and it shall burn and devour his thorns and his briers in one day;*

*And shall consume the glory of his forest, and of his fruitful field, both soul and body: and they shall be as when a standard- bearer fainteth.*

*And the rest of the trees of his forest shall be few, that a child may write them."*

**Isaiah 10:16-19**

*"Behold, the Lord maketh the earth empty, and maketh it waste, and turneth it upside down, and scattereth abroad the inhabitants thereof.*

*And it shall be, as with the people, so with the priest; as with the servant, so with his master; as with the maid, so with her mistress;*

139

*as with the buyer, so with the seller; as with the lender, so with the borrower; as with the taker of usury, so with the giver of usury to him.*

*The land shall be utterly emptied, and utterly spoiled: for the Lord hath spoken this word.*

*The earth mourneth and fadeth away, the world languisheth and fadeth away, the haughty people of the earth do languish.*

*The earth also is defiled under the inhabitants thereof; because they have transgressed the laws, changed the ordinance, broken the everlasting covenant.*

*Therefore hath the curse devoured the earth, and they that dwell therein are desolate: therefore the inhabitants of the earth are burned, and few men left."*

*"From the uttermost part of the earth have we heard songs, even glory to the righteous. But I said, My leanness, my leanness, woe unto me! The treacherous dealers have dealt treacherously; yea, the treacherous dealers have dealt very treacherously.*

*Fear, and the pit, and the snare, are upon thee, O inhabitant of the earth.*

*And it shall come to pass, that he who fleeth from the noise of the fear shall fall into the pit; and he that cometh up out of the midst of the pit shall be taken in the snare: for the windows from on high are open, and foundations of the earth do shake.*

*The earth is utterly broken down, the earth is clean dissolved, the earth is moved exceedingly.*

*The earth shall reel to and fro like a drunkard, and shall be removed like a cottage; and the transgression thereof shall be heavy upon it; and it shall fall, and not rise again.*

*And it shall come to pass in that day, that the Lord shall punish the host of the high ones that are on high, and the kings of the earth upon the earth."*

**Isaiah 24:1-6, 16-21**

*"For behold, the day cometh, that shall burn as an oven: and all the proud, yea, and all that do wickedly, shall be stubble: and the day that cometh shall burn them up, saith the Lord of hosts, that it shall leave them neither root nor branch.*

*But unto you that fear my name shall the Sun of righteousness arise with healing in his wings: and ye shall go forth, and grow up as calves of the stall."*

**Malachi 4:1-2**

From the above prophetic verses, we see that Peter based his visionary thoughts upon the truth of the words of Isaiah the Prophet. Peter was not heralding a new concept; he was merely echoing his faith in the prophecies. We find the Holy One of Israel addressing the arrogance of haughty, boastful Euro-gentiles while reminding them that there is another element that views them in all of their splendor only as a grain of sand on the seashore.

God's fire is His word. For only His word can destroy the devil. Heat, fire and smoke that consume the wicked is Truth, light, righteousness, etc. Moreover, it produces a heavenly state of existence.

In contrast, devil's fire or hellfire creates an evil state of existence. The fear, anxiety and frustration that stalks the earth today is the hellfire of the devil. Hatred, wickedness, perversion, racism, selfishness and all of the other negatives that prevail in the wicked societies of the world are the devil's arsenal to retain his constituency in a continuous state of pandemonium!

In Euro-gentile theological folklore, we find the devil in a place called Hades (hell) surrounded by flames of fire. He has pitchfork in hand and is clad in what seems to be a fireproof suit. He seems to be giving the impression that either fire can't consume him or that he has overcome its singes. All of those he forks in seem to also fare well in hell's fire, as if they've been well-trained in what to expect; only be sure to pick up your red, fireproof garment. My question is one that is probably seldom asked and possibly never considered: Is the fire his friend or enemy? Did he start it or merely adjust to it out of necessity? Why has the devil been portrayed as living in fire instead of possibly dying in the fire? The

## The Elements (Shall Melt from Intensive Heat)

Prophet Isaiah insists that God would kindle a fire in the habitation of the wicked. Just like the folklore image, you and all the earth's inhabitants are perishing by the tens of thousands daily, weekly, monthly and annually in the devil's fire (the state of existence under evil rulership) but it appears that you've been deceived to believe it is just normal. You take the devil's fire and the foul smell of smoke (the pollutants, contaminants, impurities, etc.) as evidence of progress instead of a process of destruction. Hell on earth has been made a living adventure, a preferred habitation of the sons of darkness. Where are the Sons of Light? Wherever they are, if they are regaining their Godly consciousness, they are trying to and struggling to escape the hell in which they have been trapped since their fall. By their works you shall know them.

When man fell into sin, initially a low temperature fire was kindled to warn and make some aware of the dangers of playing with and in fire. After which, this fire steadily increased in intensity and temperature as generations passed, making it more and more risky and destructive, culminating in the consumptive destruction of all these that refused to respond to God's word and seek another dwelling place. The final destruction for this age will come during a time prophetically called "Judgment Day", or "The Day of the Lord". After this judgment, the Sons of Light will reign during a peaceful rectification and restoration of the planet earth. Those of the earth's destroyers that remain alive will be compelled to live in an atmosphere which is contrary to their composition, with men of God. That is, as the Sons of Light have suffered in their hellish societies, so shall the earth's destroyers suffer in a heavenly abode. A seal will be put upon them so that all that pass by may know them as the former destroyers of the habitation of men. Their wings of deception shall be clipped. They will be trapped beyond a great gulf as the rich man that disinherited Lazarus; their souls irreparable. They shall exist in a realm called Everlasting Torment according to the spirit of the Sons of Light. They will bear witness to the rise of African Americans and others of their so-called Third World. The process of undoing all of the damage done by evil, satanic elements will be long and tedious. However, the Children of Light have been allotted one thousand years of peace and harmony to make the way straight by removing all obstacles that were placed before men by the spirit of err - satan.

In the world of err, the path was very broad, with so many diversified but accepted ways, while in the Kingdom of God, the path is straight and the lanes very narrow, with only one way to enter. With the establishment of the Kingdom of God, the Children of Israel have been gathered in both body and spirit to reign over or to head the Council of Righteousness. The principal characters chosen for this monumental task will be those who have returned from the exile and were formerly called African Americans. Men from the ends of the earth will come up to Jerusalem to receive the instructions of the God of Jacob, the one God of Creation. They will start their ascension from religion and graduate into righteousness. They shall learn and teach; they shall desire war no more.

A thousand years in God's sanctuary after descending to the brink of total destruction may seem as if it is a long period of time. But after thoroughly considering the devastating effect that evil has wrought upon the composition of man's soul, it won't seem so long. Presently, humanity has not even begun to consider the devastation caused by Euro-gentile dominion, accompanied by a complete collapse of institutions and the consequences thereof. Just the thought of surviving becomes an awesome task, not to mention the process of reconstructing religion; religion must undergo a process of renewal, repair and reconsideration. After the one thousand years have expired, the spirit of satan, of err, of opposition to good, right and God, will be released and inspire a rebellion amongst the former destroyers of the earth located geographically in a place in Europe called Gog and Magog[1].

They will attempt to reassert themselves as a power to be reckoned with and demand a return to the freedom of the damned. It is at that time that satan will meet his final and total destruction. He will be cast into a place envisioned in the Hebrew mind called a lake of fire and brimstone along with the beast and false religion. Let us all cry out "Halleluyah, Halleluyah, Halleluyah" to the one God that made Heaven and Earth who has remembered and fulfilled His word spoken by His messengers, the prophets.

---

[1] The northern region of Europe and Russia

Now let us return briefly to the fire of hell - the abode of the wicked. How did the fire get kindled and who kindled it? For it is written, "Behold the Lord God will do nothing but He would reveal His secrets of what has to be done to His servants the prophets." (Amos 3:6) The fire was started by and is being maintained and increased by evil locked in a struggle against right. It's like going against the grain, or going north when south is the proper way to travel. Thereby, friction is created. Everything that God created was good and right. The Law and Order of His universe is perfect. Every attempt to circumvent that Law and Order creates friction.

FRICTION is:    (1) The clashing between two persons or parties of opposed views.

                (2) Resistance to relative motion by two bodies in contact. Example: a match bursts in flames when heated through friction.

The Word of God is fire; it opposes all evil. If an individual is corrected because of his offense and he submits willingly to the admonishment, the words of God will then purge or purify. However, if he rebels, friction is created to burn by hook or crook the sin from the soul. Wherefore, arrogance, stiff-neckedness and stubbornness are sure creators of friction because the Word of God, being all-powerful, will either purify the soul or consume it. Thus, obedience is better than sacrifice. To oppose the Word of God is suicidal because the ultimate end of all opposers of God's Word is torment in the fire and finally, death.

Throughout the message of the inspired prophets, we find the Word of God being referred to as fire. This fire in most instances is of dual purpose. To purge and purify is one and if you remain in a state of sin too long it will destroy. When the initial hellfire was started, it was to make men aware of their dangerous environment, to purge them so that they would not descend into God's purifying fires of chastisement. The arch adversary of God, satan, has made himself very comfortable in the fire. He even showed forth his continuity of purpose, boasting that he would make men curse God from the fire and love the darkness of hell rather than to seek God and escape according to His plan. The devil

144

was even too arrogant to feign dead. He seemed to be having fun in the fire, burning, yet faring well. Satan has caused the desires and preferences of men to be his hellfire - diversity, perverseness, contrariness, etc. For example, God gave us fresh air to breathe into our lungs. Man, under the evil influence of the devil, has polluted, contaminated and stained the very oxygen that was created to sustain us. Yet, this process of deterioration was too slow for the devil, so he consequently devised a plan to hasten man's destruction. He imparted into man's mind the vision to create the cigarette, which ultimately sped up the process of annihilation.

The Sons of God were preaching the good tidings of the Kingdom of Heaven and the devil's constituency was not even deterred from openly flaunting fire-proof suits, dancing to his tune and stating: "This hell is the best thing that ever happened to us." Nevertheless, their evil deeds intensified the friction.

The knowing fool does not understand what it takes to make him wise. The wise must suffer that the unwise be saved. The fool suffers nothing. The merciful must suffer the deeds of the fool that he be saved. My God, my God, help me to teach this Truth comprehensively today, that thy people and all humanity may see the lies and deception of what they were taught yesterday!

We may ascertain at this time with relative ease that the Word of God, Truth, is a combustible material. When it is opposed, it creates heat through friction; subsequently, this heat ignites into flames of fire. Peter said the elements will be destroyed from intense heat. With the coming of the Kingdom of God and subsequent formulation of the doctrine of the Kingdom, the open struggle between the two opposing forces was made manifest.

*"Who among you will give ear to this? Who will hearken and hear for the time to come?*

*Who gave Jacob for a spoil, and Israel to the robbers? Did not the Lord, he against whom we sinned? For they would not walk in his ways neither were they obedient unto his law.*

## The Elements (Shall Melt from Intensive Heat)

*Therefore, he hath poured upon him the fury of his anger, and the strength of battle; and it hath set him on fire round about, yet he knew not; and it burned him, yet he laid it not to heart."*

Isaiah 42: 23-25

"What is the true spiritual significance of the return of the Sons of God? The return of the Children of Israel and the subsequent establishing of the Kingdom of God signalled the end of Euro-gentile dominion over God's creation and people. The Euro-gentile society or world is off its axis, reeling to and fro under the mighty hand of God's judgment. There will never be a return to the former prosperity of what was called the "good ole days". The Word of God and the entire planetary force have combined forces to bring about instability, hostility, anxiety and fear in all countries of the world.

The Word of God is the major destabilizer, bringing all evil doctrine into judgment. Nature and the elements are again coming under the rule of the Sons of God. The authority is first meted out in small portions in the season of the test; whereas after showing themselves to be steadfast in Truth and dedication to God, all things will be given back into the hands of the Sons as it was in the beginning.

### God the Black Man and Truth

Before the coming of the Kingdom of God there were men who provided a small ray of light; they did not bow to Baal but instead kept the fire kindled. Thanks be unto God for those that would not let the light be extinguished, although beleaguered by a volley of lies.

Then in 1967, we entered the prophetic season of time called "The Day of the Lord", which coincided with the Sons of Light being set in motion to establish the prophesied Kingdom of God. This motion from death to life and shame to glory was opposed by the sons of darkness, creating more friction and thus more heat upon the opposers. From the seed of the woman (people) that escaped, a Messianic man-child was to be born whose mission it would be to establish the Kingdom of God. Satan attempted to destroy the woman (people) that had escaped to the wilderness of Liberia. (Read The Impregnable People by Prince Gavriel HaGadol.) But God helped them to survive the great opposition to

146

their upward motion. There was more friction and more intensive heat in hell from the combustible Truth - the Word of God.

*"And when the dragon saw that he was cast unto the earth, he persecuted the woman which brought forth the man child.*

*And to the woman were given two wings of a great eagle, that she might fly into the wilderness, into her place, where she is nourished for a time, and times, and half a time, from the face of the serpent.*

*And the serpent cast out of his mouth water as a flood after the woman, that he might cause her to be carried away by the flood.*

*And the earth helped the woman, and the earth opened her mouth, and swallowed up the flood which the dragon cast out of his mouth.*

*And the dragon was wroth with the woman, and went to make war with the remnant of her seed, which keep the commandments of God, and have the testimony of Jesus Christ."*

**Revelations 12:13-17**

With the establishing of the Kingdom of God, the opposition of the adversaries of God to the coming of His Kingdom caused the Euro-gentile world to plunge into an irreversible state of decadence. Since 1967, decadence and perversion of every form have increased: drug usage, promiscuity, homosexuality, family instability, unwed motherhood, sexual perversion. The list is enormous. Now each attempt to destroy the Kingdom of God and its credibility causes further destruction for the perpetrator; the more the opposition to Truth, the greater the friction. The greater the friction, the greater the indignation of the flames of hell. God's adversary throws sand in my eyes and blinds himself.

The Day of Atonement 1970, the historical date on which God's Kingdom was officially established on earth, created a greater intensity of heat. The Day of Atonement (also known as Yom Kippur) is the highest holy day of the Hebrew nation which falls during the Fall of the year. This holy day was designated to make amends for the sins committed during the previous year. Also, it marks the beginning of the spiritual new year according to the will and plan of God. This is for all men, though most do not yet understand its significance. Any new world order would have to have its beginning after the spiritual purification of the Day of Atonement. This starts man's new beginning at peace and in oneness with God. This event (the establishment of the Kingdom of God) was of major prophetic importance. Principally at the forefront of this move were the Children of Israel, but blessings would be reaped by all of the earth's people. This Kingdom's establishment was in fulfillment of Daniel 2:44. This epoch signalled the inevitable decline of the Euro-gentile dominion. It will eventually have even greater spiritual and historical significance as men seek to chart the exact time that the Euro-gentile dominion began its fall. These two opposing views or forces were made manifest by God in order to give man his final choice. The alternative had come as prophesied and promised. The mustard seed Kingdom had emerged in the appointed place at the appointed time. Though the mustard be the smallest of seeds, it would nevertheless become the greatest tree of the forest, providing nourishment and shelter to all that hunger and thirst for a change.

When the seed of the Kingdom was planted by God, it needed much tender care. When a seed is first planted, it is not seen by all that pass by. The first growth is downward, not upward. It has to take root. The strong root will have to provide the lifeline for the plant at every stage of its development. The rooting time is of greater importance; it is an unseen time of consideration and personal communication between seed and planter. The more care, the deeper and stronger the root. The strong roots would aid the tender plant to withstand the coming frost and heat. Like the seedling, the coming of the Kingdom of God (the moment of splendor) was not recognized or fully appreciated. Many of its young citizens were perplexed as to their roles and calling. The Kingdom had come but they saw no outward change in their lives. Nevertheless, as they would soon comprehend, their lives, nor anyone else's would ever be the same. They had no problem believing that it was certainly God's Kingdom, for they saw nothing for themselves.

I received the vision to establish the Kingdom of God as I lay upon my bed in the year 1966, the month of October, on the Day of Atonement. The Word of God came unto me. He declared, "You must return to Israel to establish my Kingdom on earth. You must go via West Africa. There you and your congregation must sojourn for an outer perimeter of time of three and one-half years, wherein you shall fulfill the Prophecy of Ezekiel 20:33, 38. You shall leave America in the year 1967. After the fulfilling of the time allotted to remain in West Africa, you shall proceed on to the Holy Land. You must be in Israel by the Day of Atonement 1970 to begin the last week of Daniel's prophecy (a similitude) and to establish the Kingdom of God which shall be in its glory by the year 1977."

Since the Coming of the Vision to establish the Kingdom of God, cycles of time have been measured in periods of either seven years or three and one-half years. With the passing of each cycle, the Sons of Light and the sons of darkness would intensify their struggle. The more contact, the more friction. The increased friction caused greater discomfort in hell (America, Europe, and throughout the world) as the temperature of the flames continued to rise.

> *"Then I said, I will not make mention of him, nor speak any more in his name. But his word was in mine heart like a burning fire shut up in my bones, and I was weary with forbearing, and I could not stay."*
>
> **Jeremiah 20:9**

> *"I said I will take heed to my ways, that I sin not with my tongue: I will keep my mouth with a bridle, while the wicked is before me.*
>
> *I was dumb with silence, I held my peace, even from good; and my sorrow was stirred.*
>
> *My heart was hot within me, while I was musing the fire burned: then spoke I with my tongue."*
>
> **Psalms 39:1-3**

Moving under the shield of the God of Israel, though we were 350 neophytes from the ghettoes of Chicago, Cleveland, Detroit, etc. with

149

regard to the proper usage of the higher spiritual forces, we listened and were faithful to the Word of God as it was revealed in the midst of us. We proceeded as instructed: Take seven years to re-establish the sanctuary - God's stronghold - Jerusalem. Rebuild "the street and the wall" (reinstitute moral law and true worship), even during troublous times. The sanctuary was the temple within us in our midst and in our hearts. The street (the highway of the Lord) was to be the path for all those that sought the True God and an ensign for the masters (the wise men). We moved expediently and obediently to sanctify the truthful worship of God, or we could say to inaugurate true Temple Worship (See "The True Worship of God", <u>God, the Black Man and Truth</u>) for the days of the Kingdom.

The uniting of Jerusalem (prior to the Six Day War, Jerusalem was divided into two sections - East Jerusalem, which was controlled by Jordan, and West Jerusalem which was under Jewish authority) was sanctioned by our/the Kingdom being set in motion at Passover 1967. Our motion was the spiritual force behind the success of the Six Day War because the unification of Jerusalem was a prerequisite for the establishing of the Kingdom of God and the beginning of the Messianic Process of Deliverance for all men from the yoke of Euro-gentile economic and social strangulation. The fire that was released by our acceptance of our moral responsibility to humanity activated the process of destruction of the satanic forces and the purification of the earth. The wall - law, instructions - was to provide a shield of truth in order to strengthen those whom the evil one has silenced. The masters that have had their words and wisdom imprisoned by the opposing forces must now be resurrected, for there has to be contact between the words of Truth and the lies of destruction that have ploughed up the way back unto God. No man of Truth can remain silent during the Messianic Age. Without friction, the hand of evil is strengthened.

*"I have set watchmen upon thy walls, O Jerusalem, which shall never hold their peace day nor night: ye that make mention of the Lord, keep not silence,*

*And give him no rest, till he establish, and till he make Jerusalem a praise in the earth."*

*"Go through, go through the gates: prepare ye the way of the people; cast up, cast up the highway; gather out the stones; lift up a standard for the people.*

*Behold the Lord hath proclaimed unto the end of the world, Say ye to the daughter of Zion, Behold, thy salvation cometh; behold, his reward is with him, and his work before him."*

**Isaiah 62:6-7, 10-11**

*"And shall say, Cast ye up, cast ye up, prepare the way, take up the stumbling block out of the way of my people.*

*For thus saith the high and lofty One that inhabiteth eternity, whose name is Holy; I dwell in the high and holy place, with him also that is of a contrite and humble spirit, to revive the spirit of the humble, and to revive the heart of the contrite ones."*

**Isaiah 57:14-15**

Who shall believe the report and to whom has God given ears to hear? We did develop before God into a tender plant, as a shoot out of what appeared to be dry, fallow ground. We were despised and rejected of men; we met sorrow and became acquainted with grief. All people hid their faces from us. We were dejected and not esteemed.

The Children of Israel of the North American captivity are like unto their fathers in ancient Egypt who did not appreciate the signs and wonders wrought by Moses. They, like the African American today, being flesh and blood and void of spirit, could not grasp or believe God moving through their lives. Moreover, who would believe that a group of Black Biblical Israelites, remnants of chattel slaves though minuscule in number, are presently in the Holy Land fulfilling prophecies, activating God's word and unleashing the corrective forces upon the world and all of its inhabitants? The people that have been walking in darkness have seen a great light. They that have been dwelling on this planet earth in the shadow (darkness) of death, upon them hath the light shined. The glorious Kingdom confirmed the re-establishing of man's spiritual center at Jerusalem, the city of Peace. The law (instructions) will now go forth from Zion and the Truth from Jerusalem.

151

# The Elements (Shall Melt from Intensive Heat)

The next historic event commenced during the season of Passover 1974 - The Midst of the Week, or half of the seven-year allotted time - in which there was a systematic method of deportations employed against us by the powers that be to obstruct the rhythm of the formulation of the New Covenant; this was the agreement between the Holy One of Israel and those of the exiles that had returned to Jerusalem, according to His will, to make reconciliation for iniquity and to worship Him in His Holy Mountain.

Under this New Covenant, He would put His instructions (law) in our inward parts and write it upon our hearts, guiding us to understanding the law as it was to be in the days of the Kingdom of God. We would grow from the same root as Moses; there would be no conflict or denial of His inspired direction. We were made the pruners of the vine, removing old branches, dressing the tree so that the same fruit is produced, yet stronger. We've pruned to protect the growth so that the tree would not be destroyed. The law that gives us the insight into God's thinking and will is a blessing, for it is like a blueprint to guide us in building His Holy habitation in our hearts and homes. As we abide by this New Covenant, we are neither selfish nor arrogant. Our love for Moses is perfect; he is an everlasting symbol of Godliness imbued in our hearts and minds.

There is nothing that we personally or selfishly desire to change or remove from the Law. We leave God's will as the determining factor and His choice as our command. We neither add to or take away. With all of our hearts, soul and might we endeavor to fulfill the will of the Omnipotent, Most Holy God of Creation. I have made mention of these historical confrontations and moments of splendor because they have influenced the progressive destruction of the dominion of the Euro-gentiles. Each contact is significant because the fire has to be heated seven times over. It is during the seventh elevation of degrees that God will end this era of rule by men that are bound under satanic influence.

Nebuchadnezzar, the King of Babylon, heated the fire seven times in his attempt to destroy the three Hebrews: Hananiah, Mishael and Azariah. They perished not, for the Heavenly Father did deliver them from the hands of death that had tormented their souls as the adversary of God tried to kill them. So likewise, by fire shall those evil tormentors meet their end.

> *"Then was Nebuchadnezzar full of fury, and the form of his visage was changed against Shadrach, Meshach, and Abed-nego: therefore he spoke, and commanded that they should heat the furnace seven times more than it was wont to be heated.*
>
> *And he commanded the most mighty men that were in his army to bind Shadrach, Meshach, and Abed-nego, and to cast them into the burning fiery furnace.*
>
> *Then these men were bound in their coats, their hosen, and their hats, and their other garments, and were cast into the midst of the burning fiery furnace."*
>
> **Daniel 3: 19-21**

> *"And render unto our neighbors sevenfold into their bosom their reproach, wherewith they have reproached thee, O Lord."*
>
> **Psalms 79:12**

> *"When I thought to know this, it was too painful for me.*
>
> *Until I went into the sanctuary of God; then understood I their end."*
>
> **Psalms 73:16-17**

The light of Israel shall be for fire and His Holy One for a flame. The spiritual and intellectual growth of the Sons of Light shall continue to increase, while their relationship with God becomes stronger and stronger. This intellectual army of God shall burn and devour satan's briars and thorns in one day...The Day of the Lord. The former Heavens and earth are passing away; this world is presently in a period of transition. Many inhabitants of the earth have grown weary of evil societies and evil systems. The yearn for change is stronger than ever before; they are overcoming the fear to speak out against and confute that which is deadly wrong.

The next elevation of intensity was at the Day of Atonement 1977, the Sealed New Covenant, which marked another level of our elevation and intensification of the heat. This signalled a new era entitled, "The Kingdom of God in its Glory". This was the beginning of the fourth heat increase, with three more still to come. The Glory of the Kingdom moved us from formulation to preachment, from an unseen seed to a tender shoot; i.e., we became more active and visible and the Divine Presence of God became more obvious.

In the forthcoming days, months and years, the Kingdom will continue to grow and develop and all peoples, nations and things that will be enjoined to it will bear witness that the root that had developed during the formative years was the cause. And God spoke through the prophet Jeremiah: "Set up a standard in the land, blow ye the trumpet among the nations for thou (The Kingdom of God) has become my battle ax and weapon of war: For with thee will I break in pieces the right of wrong to rule." To exploit and destroy will no longer be a privilege but a crime. And we, being armed with the Omnipotent Word of God, are authorized to bring all criminals before the Judgment Bar of God Almighty.

We understood that in order to keep the flames ignited, we had to continuously reveal and challenge the force of evil. We are the candle that had been lit by God and placed on top of the Mountain to give light (intellect) unto all of those in darkness (ignorance). Gradually we've evolved into Sainthood. As our God-works are made manifest before men, let them give all praises unto the Holy One of Israel. Isaiah had told us to "rise and shine". (Isaiah 60:1-2) In our obedience to God's Plan, we were confronted many times by duplicitous individuals professing to be religious but who preferred not to hear or remember the Word of God. Nevertheless, the evil elements were burning, whether you were Black or White, Gentile or atheist. The choice was clear: change or perish. Wickedness shall be destroyed by fire, which is kindled by the Word of God. No other process will work.

How do we become experts in the usage of the Word of God? It's simple. We must study.

*"The Lord is exalted: for he dwelleth on high: he hath filled Zion with judgement and righteousness.*

*And wisdom and knowledge shall be the stability of thy times, and strength of salvation: the fear of the Lord is his treasure."*

**Isaiah 33:5-6**

We now find Isaiah admonishing us to study. For wisdom and knowledge will become the key to survival in the Day of the Lord. The study to which I'm referring is not the higher education found in worldly institutions, but it is a call for a Renaissance of study and interest in the law and inspired words of the Prophets of God.

The basis for the new direction (element) that is needed in government, society, culture and family can only be found in the light (intellect) of God's Holy words. All men desiring that the light of God be shone upon their path should be engulfed in Biblical, life-related, righteous study, seeking their salvation and once found, share the plan of salvation with others. Who amongst the nations shall be able to survive the devouring fire? Wherefore, let your first desire be my words; desire them and you shall be instructed. For the Holy One of Israel, which is Lord over all, shall fear no man's person, neither shall He stand in awe of any man's greatness. It is time to set thine heart and mind upon the ordinances of God and meditate continually in His commandments; the Most High God shall establish thine heart and give thee wisdom to escape the damnation of hell.

*"Thou has plotted shame to thy house by cutting off many peoples, and hast sinned against thy soul.*

*For the stone shall cry out of the wall, and the beam out of the timber shall answer it.*

*Woe to him that buildeth a town with blood, and establisheth a city by iniquity!*

## The Elements (Shall Melt from Intensive Heat)

*Behold, it is not of the Lord of hosts that the people shall labor in the very fire, and the people shall weary themselves for nothing?*

*For the earth shall be filled with the knowledge of the glory of the Lord, as the waters cover the sea."*

**Habakkuk 2: 10-14**

My primary objective is that you, the reader, be made consciously aware that you are living in The Day of the Lord, though I must be circumspect and admonish you not to attempt to calculate or formulate an exact day and hour of the consummation of this season of compounded destruction. No man knows the day and hour - only the Father which dwells in the Heavens. God, in His infinite wisdom, has sought out the thoughts of man, whereas if he knew or could determine the day and hour, he would repent with all obvious sincerity the day before. It is for that reason that the end of this world can only be revealed and preached by the season. Therefore, the Saints of the Most High God do preach the end of this age by faith. I therefore admonish you to take heed to the things that are occurring; they do testify to this being the end of Esau and the rise of Jacob. (Esau signifies the end of this world and Jacob is the beginning of the world to come. II Esdras 6:9, the Apocrypha) How can you be sure? You can't be sure without faith. You must believe and activate the works of salvation which will be the testimony of your faith.

Reflecting back to the Bible, I call your attention to the term "The Olivet Discourse". The Olivet Discourse was a very somber lesson taught by Yeshua (Jesus) of Nazareth to His disciples on the Mount of Olives in Jerusalem. This outstanding discourse described a series of events, prophecies and manifestations, signifying the end of this age and/or this world. Here the Apostles approached Yeshua (Jesus) and asked the questions: "Tell us: when shall these things be? What shall be the sign of thy coming and the consummation of the age?" His initial response was to admonish them to pay attention and beware of those who would come referring to him as the Greek Christ(os) to deceive many. Here we note Yeshua (Jesus) warning and complaining of being conceptualized as the Christ(os). Perhaps there are a vast number of individual offenders guilty of this trespass but to bring individual

156

trespassers to justice would be like plucking leaves off a giant oak tree; we best examine the roots of the entire tree that bears the branches and leaves. In this case, the principle offender that has and continues to deceive many concerning his Messianic calling is the apostate church, to which we are a witness. The apostate church, misusing His teachings, has lured the masses onto a path of confusion and deception. Should this be an issue to debate? Other than in contemporary Euro-gentile Christianity, in what other areas do we find widespread deception surrounding this Messianic personage? The answer being obvious, what are the areas of confusion and deception?

The confusion stems from the fact that within Euro-gentile Christian religions there are numerous beliefs and concepts. The multifarious religions advocate that their version or manner of worship is proper and right (each representing a false Christ(os)). Do you recall that the Catholic religion is the root of the Evangelistic Christian religion? Within the ranks of Catholicism was discontent and a protest was made which gave birth to the Protestant Church. From that stemmed the Baptists. Afterwards a new method was devised which provoked the formulation of the Methodist Church. The list goes on and on.

*"Then if anyone says to you, 'Behold, here is the Christ,' or 'There He is,' do not believe him.*

*For false Christs and false prophets will arise and will show great signs and wonders, so as to mislead, if possible, even elect.*

*Behold, I have told you in advance."*

**St. Matthew 24: 23-25**
**Hebrew-Greek Key Study Bible**

The God of Israel states emphatically that He is a God that changes not. This being the case, where is the confusion in God's word? Yeshua (Jesus) said that not a dot from the I or cross from the T should be taken away from the law. So where is the duplicity? Yeshua (Jesus) himself was not deceptive nor his words confusing. Only the misconceptions, misunderstandings and deceptive explanations of his sayings within the Euro-gentile concepts of Christianity are deceptive and confusing.

## The Elements (Shall Melt from Intensive Heat)

What was in its inception a very sound doctrine, somewhere through the annals of time came under the influence of that evil element which had disguised itself as a vessel of light. It was also taught that there would be wars and rumors of war, presaging a world of strife and contention and intractable situations born out of greed and misappropriation of the earth's wealth. A world was created that makes war with God while advocating Peace, manufacturing weapons and products of environmental destruction to protect the earth's people. Yet, being truthful, have all of the accumulated weapons of mass destruction given you a feeling of security, or anxiety? Wouldn't you feel better if such awesome weapons didn't exist?

Be sober minded; reject ignorance of the plan of God and forsake what is wrong. Isn't it clearly evident that the flask containing this world's sins is running over? The messengers of God have been instructed to blow the trumpet in and from God's Holy habitation, to sound a warning to the forces of evil and the earth's deceived inhabitants. The plagues and events termed "the wrath of God" have begun their descension upon this world. Certainly there is much false comfort in believing that life will go on as usual without cataclysmic changes. Yet, the final judgment is as certain as the arrogance of the denuded world leaders. Only if we negate the existence of the true and living God can we propose that the multitude of Euro-American and Euro-gentile atrocities and international crimes will go unpunished.

Yeshua (Jesus) also spoke of the captivity of the Messianic Nation, exhorting them to endure persecution and abasement. Yet, when the word of God goes forth, they shall become the first fruit of God's salvation. They shall gather around God's throne to be fashioned into the instruments through which the Messiah extends God's salvation unto all men. They shall rule with the Anointed and teach under him in the days of the Kingdom of God. They shall establish the infrastructure of Divine government that will be emulated by all nations upon the face of God's earth.

Another event spoken of was the heralding of a doctrine called "The Gospel of the Kingdom of God". It is understandable that before there could be a gospel or good news of the Kingdom, it would have to be preceded by the Kingdom being established. Daniel gave us the precise time of the establishing of this Kingdom spoken of by Yeshua (Jesus). First, Europe would be in the process of developing its economic zenith through continental unity. This organization of European nations is presently called the "European Common Market". This particular entity seems harmless enough because it was supposedly formed primarily to expedite more efficiently its goods and services, but its true objectives are far more ominous to this planet and people. However, according to Daniel's prophecy, this was to be the last and final form of a Gentile world power structure. The outstanding difference would be that this time God's Kingdom would be in existence as the God-inspired alternative. They both would exist simultaneously during the same period of time. Immediately after the statement on the Kingdom, Yeshua (Jesus) directs us to the book of the Prophet Daniel for further clarity of events.

*"And in the days of these kings shall the God of heaven set up a kingdom, which shall never be destroyed: and the kingdom shall not be left to other people, but it shall break in pieces and consume all these kingdoms, and it shall stand for ever."*

**Daniel 2:44**

*"But as the days of Noah were, so shall also the coming of the Son of man be.*

*For as in the days that were before the flood they were eating and drinking, marrying and giving in marriage, until the day that Noah entered into the ark.*

*And knew not until the flood came, and took them all away; so shall also the coming of the Son of man be."*

**St. Matthew 24:37-39**
**INCORRECT TRANSLATION**

*"As in the days of Noah thus shall it also be at the coming of the Son of Man.*

*For while in the days of the (first) flood, they were eating and drinking, marrying and consenting to marriage until the day Noah entered the ark.*

*And they were not knowledgeable until the (second) flood came and destroyed all of them. Thus it shall also be at the coming of the Son of Man."*

St. Matthew 24:37-39<br>CORRECT INTERPRETATION

*"And God saw that the wickedness of man was great in the earth, and that every imagination of the thoughts of his heart was only evil continually."*

*"The earth also was corrupt before God, and the earth was filled with violence.*

*And God looked upon the earth, and, behold, it was corrupt; for all flesh had corrupted his way upon the earth.*

*And God said unto Noah, The end of all flesh is come before me; for the earth is filled with violence through them; and, behold, I will destroy them with the earth."*

Genesis 6:5, 11-13

Yeshua (Jesus) also gives us very vivid insight as to the state of mind and affairs of the world while the doctrine of the Kingdom is being taught.

After close perusal of the Hebrew scriptures, we find the King James version of "as in the days of Noah," to be very misleading. First, there is no word "before" in the Hebrew text. It would be self-evident what the inhabitants of the earth were doing before the flood. The Truth is that there were two floods mentioned by Yeshua (Jesus). This is the same type of similitude used by God in forecasting the pending destruction of modern Babylonian societies. To observe the first destruction requires consciousness and faith in the Deliverer and the Deliverance. With its advent comes a plan of escape, even as Noah brought, and the Kingdom is bringing at this very moment. This is the time during which the people must hear and believe. Yeshua (Jesus) said that the inhabitants of this world would have the same opportunity to be saved as they had in the days of Noah.

"When ye shall see the budding of the trees, know ye that summer is nigh. One must be cautious not to wait to see this "budding" (the wrath of God and impending destruction of the Euro-gentile world) with the natural eye. In order to be saved from this fate, one must hear the plane engines roaring and see the bombs falling <u>before</u> the actual event takes place. To wait to receive a visual confirmation of such an event with the natural eye would be tantamount to suicide! There are always two immutable things: a thought or vision (the spiritual) which is soon followed by the <u>substance</u> of that thought or vision (the physical). The first destruction of America is the spiritual destruction which is seen with the spiritual senses of the "God Mind." This destruction must be seen in a spiritual vision in order that men might be saved by coming out of that world. It has to be preached and acted upon just as if the event was actually taking place. You recall that Noah moved by faith to build the ark many years prior to the sighting of the first rain. Yet this spiritual vision (coupled with his faith and works), enabled him to escape the coming destruction.

God makes known His plans to His servants, who then warn the people of the apparent danger and give instructions as to what they must do to escape the wrath of God Almighty."

<u>God the Black Man and Truth</u>

Yeshua (Jesus) is thus warning us of the imminent dangers of arrogant, haughty spirits. The clarity of the two floods mentioned is thus: Noah preached salvation during the first flood which was a flood of iniquity. The earth had sunk under the weight of corruption and man's self-confidence in his own abilities as master of the earth. Therefore, as Noah taught, there was complete apathy; they continued to party, buy, sell, build, marry and divorce - business as usual. They believed not until the second flood of waters came and swept them away. Noah preached for forty years without finding even one adherent to the faith - a very evil generation indeed. So shall it be at the coming of the Son

161

of Man. He would begin his mission at the time of the great falling away from God and there would be no great interest in His way of life.

Again, take heed as with Lazarus and the non-repentant rich man. There are set times for repentance; no one knows the seasons' end but the Heavenly Father. Yet, He does reveal His will to His servants.

Euro-gentile religion has made man very comfortable in sin. People are no longer circumspect of the things they say and do. Everyone that is a victim of subliminal deception feels they have forever to make the required changes. Yet in truth, those that are in search of God must choose Him while there is still a definite choice between good and evil, God and satan. You cannot just come to God because there is nothing else left; thereby, He merely wins by forfeit. Turn unto God while you have liberty and there is yet a place of repentance open unto you.

After Noah completed his preachment, he departed from his people's midst that last evening or morning, as he had done on many other occasions. Only God knew that day that He would not be returning. I'm certain that He had said on many occasions, "one day you'll look for me and I'll be gone." Noah was moved by God to enter the ark.

Once he was secured at his station, the rain began to fall, the first rain from above. And after the first full day, many were inquiring as to the whereabouts of the man called Noah. They just wanted to see his face. After another full wet day, there were some ready to repent; the number increased with the depth of the water. But it was too late; they were trapped in everlasting torment. Their minds were steadfastly on evil; they never changed. They had eyes but could not see an entire world submerged in evil. They had ears but could not hear truth, something that should have come naturally. They were too busy with the vanities of deception to heed God's warning from the mouth of his messenger. When what was happening dawned upon them, the Son of Man had come and gone.

What kind of faulty reasoning could they have used to reject the Man of God? Who can respond better than thou as to how they reasoned? They reasoned just like you're reasoning now. Also take heed to another definite similarity. We find that when the trial began for the earth's inhabitants in the days of Noah, man had been charged with continuous, evil imaginations: wickedness, violence and corruption. The evil was to reach such a level that just allowing it to continue would have meant extinction. That will not be the case. It will not be just left to run its own destructive course. At this time God will become the determinant of this final chapter. He will show Himself on the side of His servants and all the world shall know that the judgment is His and His alone.

Since this world is to be destroyed by fire, the destruction must be instigated or provoked by the Word of God. The Sons of God must fan the flames, causing continuous friction between the two opposing forces, good and evil. The final phase of this confrontation was set in motion with the establishment of the Kingdom of God. It represented the visible rise of the opposing force. The Kingdom of God is the battle ax or the source of Truth which is the combustible material needed to ignite the all-consuming fire. We are now observing the end of a world. The elements are dissolving from fervent heat. Truth has engaged evil in a life and death struggle.

This heaven and earth is passing away. Therefore, do not imitate the mistakes of your fathers; they made the wrong decision. Be ye faithful and wise servants, for verily I say unto you that this generation shall testify as to the truth of these words. This heaven and earth shall pass away, but my words shall not.

*****

Do not be disillusioned by the obvious pain and perils of the struggle. Forget not that we turned from God. We despised the manner by which we were to govern our inheritance. We were not circumspect; we desired to be like unto the ungodly nations round about us. Thus, we were given over into the hands of adversity. We were allowed to be like unto them.

Now we behold in sorrow our people that have been fashioned into the image of our adversaries. Whereas at this very late hour, we understand and no longer desire to be like unto them. We despise our former lusts; we loathe what we have become. We see a mind so evil that it could be compared with a cancerous, running sore. Now we desire our God-mind. We seek another place whose builder and maker is God. We desire our God-image again.

Needless to say, it is much easier said than done, for our inheritance is like unto a city built upon a very broad field. Inside there are all good things, even life everlasting. But there is but one path and it is very narrow indeed, comparable to the size of one man's body. On both sides of the path there are pitfalls and dangers, even a consuming fire on the left and deadly, stinging hornets on the right. Then there are four kinds standing before the entrance. There is he that looks into the narrow entrance laden with dangers and for the fear in his heart, he chokes the word and does not enter thereupon. Then there is he that enters thereupon and has no discipline of soul, wherefore he falls therefrom and is consumed. Then there is he that has listened somewhat but hates this world. He enters thereupon and because he has only listened somewhat, his balance is not perfect; thus, he is burned and stung sometimes but he continues on and makes it through. But he is gravely wounded. His wounds may or may not be healed. Then there is he that does not choke the word; he listens and can hear Truth and thus disciplines his soul; he hates the world and loves the Kingdom. Subsequently, he enters thereupon and walks the straight and narrow path unto his inheritance.

The entrance into the New World has been made narrow, full of sorrow, peril, travail and pain. But remember! The entrances in the beginning were wide and sure and brought forth immortal fruit. Thus if you labor not to enter therein, you can never receive those things that are in store for you. If we do not pass the dangers set before our inheritance, we shall never receive it. He that has ears to hear, let him hear. *Selah*

# Communicators Press Publishing and Distribution

To order additional books by Ben Ammi complete the order blank below and give the others to a friend or family member that they may further their understanding about God, His People and His Plan.

For more information or wholesale requests, write:
**Communicators Press, P.O. Box 26063; Washington, 20001**
Tel: (202) 291-9244; Fax: (202) 291-9149;
E-mail: dckoy@earthlink.net

## The Resurrection Series
By Ben Ammi
Check all that apply:

| Title | Cost | Qty |
|---|---|---|
| God the Black Man and Truth | $15.00 | |
| God and the Law of Relativity | $12.00 | |
| The Messiah and the End of this World | $17.00 | |
| Everlasting Life (From Thought to Reality) | $17.00 | |
| Yeshua the Hebrew Messiah or Jesus the Christian Christ? | $10.00 | |
| An Imitation of Life | $17.95 | |

Please send me the book(s) checked above at the total cost of $_____. Add $4.75 for shipping and handling (add $. 75 for each additional book).

Name: _____ _____

Address: _____

City, State, Zipcode: _____

Please complete the form above, include the proper funds and mail to:
Communicators Press, P.O. Box 26063; Washington, D.C. 20001

For Credit Card Order VISA, MASTERCARD, DISCOVER
or AMERICAN EXPRESS call (202) 291-9244.
or www.kingdomofyah.com/cpbooks/

# Communicators Press Publishing and Distribution

To order additional books by Ben Ammi complete the order blank below and give the others to a friend or family member that they may further their understanding about God, His People and His Plan.

For more information or wholesale requests, write:
**Communicators Press, P.O. Box 26063; Washington, 20001**
Tel: (202) 291-9244; Fax: (202) 291-9149;
E-mail: dckoy@earthlink.net

## The Resurrection Series
By Ben Ammi
Check all that apply:

| Title | Cost | Qty |
|---|---|---|
| God the Black Man and Truth | $15.00 | _____ |
| God and the Law of Relativity | $12.00 | _____ |
| The Messiah and the End of this World | $17.00 | _____ |
| Everlasting Life (From Thought to Reality) | $17.00 | _____ |
| Yeshua the Hebrew Messiah or Jesus the Christian Christ? | $10.00 | _____ |
| An Imitation of Life | $17.95 | _____ |

Please send me the book(s) checked above at the total cost of $_____. Add $4.75 for shipping and handling (add $. 75 for each additional book).

Name: _____     _____

Address: _____

City, State, Zipcode: _____

Please complete the form above, include the proper funds and mail to:
Communicators Press, P.O. Box 26063; Washington, D.C. 20001

For Credit Card Order VISA, MASTERCARD, DISCOVER
or AMERICAN EXPRESS call (202) 291-9244.
or www.kingdomofyah.com/cpbooks/

# Communicators Press Publishing and Distribution

To order additional books by Ben Ammi complete the order blank below and give the others to a friend or family member that they may further their understanding about God, His People and His Plan.

For more information or wholesale requests, write:
**Communicators Press, P.O. Box 26063; Washington, 20001**
Tel: (202) 291-9244; Fax: (202) 291-9149;
E-mail: dckoy@earthlink.net

## The Resurrection Series
By Ben Ammi
Check all that apply:

| Title | Cost | Qty |
|---|---|---|
| God the Black Man and Truth | $15.00 | _____ |
| God and the Law of Relativity | $12.00 | _____ |
| The Messiah and the End of this World | $17.00 | _____ |
| Everlasting Life (From Thought to Reality) | $17.00 | _____ |
| Yeshua the Hebrew Messiah or Jesus the Christian Christ? | $10.00 | _____ |
| An Imitation of Life | $17.95 | _____ |

Please send me the book(s) checked above at the total cost of $_____. Add $4.75 for shipping and handling (add $. 75 for each additional book).

Name: _____

Address: _____

City, State, Zipcode: _____

Please complete the form above, include the proper funds and mail to:
Communicators Press, P.O. Box 26063; Washington, D.C. 20001

For Credit Card Order VISA, MASTERCARD, DISCOVER
or AMERICAN EXPRESS call (202) 291-9244.
or www.kingdomofyah.com/cpbooks/